The Strategic Defense Initiative

About the Authors

STANLEY ARONOWITZ is Professor of Sociology at the Graduate Center of the City University of New York. He has participated in the founding of three schools. These include Park East High School, an experimental public high school in New York, of which he was planning director, and the Center for Worker Education at City College where he still teaches. He has authored *False Promises; Food, Shelter, and the American Dream; The Crisis in Historical Materialism; Working Class Hero;* and *The Politics of Identity.*

HENRY A. GIROUX was a secondary school teacher for seven years. He is currently the Waterbury Chair Professor at Penn State University. His books include *Ideology, Culture, and the Process of Schooling; Theory and Resistance in Education* (Bergin and Garvey, 1983); *Schooling and the Struggle for Public Life; Postmodern Education* (with Stanley Aronowitz); *Border Crossings;* and *Living Dangerously.*

About the Book and Editors

The Strategic Defense Initiative has evolved into a massively funded research and development effort with profound implications not only for weapons technology but also for East-West relations. In this volume, preeminent figures from the policymaking and and defense communities address critical aspects of the program, offering widely divergent points of view. Their essays compose an authoritative reference work on one of the major controversies of the decade.

Some contributors view SDI as the best way to develop alternatives to the strategy of retaliation by strengthening defensive deterrence, and they decry political reluctance to proceed with deployment. Others cite what they argue are virtually insurmountable technological obstacles to developing a "perfect" defense. They believe SDI will mean the end of arms control and an escalation of superpower competition in both offensive and defensive weapons.

From a foreign policy perspective, contributors examine the fear of our NATO allies that SDI represents a progressive decoupling of the U.S. strategic deterrent from the defense of Europe. As a counterpoint, it is argued that SDI is not a doctrinal revolution in American strategic policy but rather a way to gain leverage over the Soviet strategic arsenal.

Dorinda G. Dallmeyer is research director of the Dean Rusk Center for International and Comparative Law at the University of Georgia. Daniel S. Papp is director and associate professor, School of Social Sciences, Georgia Institute of Technology. He is coauthor of Communist Nations' Military Assistance (Westview, 1983).

Published in cooperation
with the Dean Rusk Center
for International and Comparative Law

The Strategic Defense Initiative

New Perspectives on Deterrence

edited by Dorinda G. Dallmeyer
in association with
Daniel S. Papp

A Dean Rusk Center Monograph

Westview Press • Boulder and London

A Dean Rusk Center Monograph

This Westview softcover edition was manufactured on our own premises using
equipment and methods that allow us to keep even specialized books in stock.
It is printed on acid-free paper and bound in softcovers that carry the highest
rating of the National Association of State Textbook Administrators, in consultation with the Association of American Publishers and the Book Manufacturers'
Institute.

Copyright © 1986 by Westview Press, Inc.

Published in 1986 in the United States of America by Westview Press, Inc.;
Frederick A. Praeger, Publisher; 5500 Central Avenue, Boulder, Colorado 80301

Library of Congress Cataloging-in-Publication Data
The Strategic defense initiative.
    (A Dean Rusk Center monograph)
    Includes index.
    1. Strategic Defense Initiative. 2. Deterrence
(Strategy) I. Dallmeyer, Dorinda G. II. Series.
UG743.S774   1986   358'.1754   86-9112
ISBN 0-8133-7238-0

Composition for this book was provided by the editor.
This book was produced without formal editing by the publisher.

Printed and bound in the United States of America

∞ The paper used in this publication meets the requirements of the
American National Standard for Permanence of Paper for Printed
Library Materials Z39.48-1984.

6 5 4 3 2

To my parents,
Betty and Hubert Gilmore,
who taught me to want to know more

Contents

PART FOUR
POLITICAL-DIPLOMATIC ISSUES

PART FIVE
CONCLUDING OBSERVATIONS

Acknowledgments

The editor accepts full responsibility for this book, but nevertheless wishes to recognize the important contributions made by others.

This book is an outgrowth of the conference "Strategic Defense: The Pros and Cons of Star Wars," co-sponsored by the Dean Rusk Center for International and Comparative Law at the University of Georgia and the School of Social Sciences at the Georgia Institute of Technology. I deeply appreciate the support of Prof. Thomas J. Schoenbaum, executive director of the Dean Rusk Center, throughout the planning of the conference. Ms. Nelda Parker of the Dean Rusk Center contributed invaluable administrative skills.

I owe a particular debt of gratitude to my counterpart at Georgia Tech, Dr. Daniel S. Papp, not only for his expertise in national security policy but also for his unfailing good humor and patience throughout the events leading up to the conference on November 15, 1985. Thanks go also to Ms. Jane Wilson of the School of Social Sciences who made the conference run smoothly.

I wish to acknowledge Dean J. Ralph Beaird, University of Georgia School of Law, and Dr. Joseph M. Pettit, president of Georgia Tech, for their financial support of the conference. Thanks also go to the W. Alton Jones Foundation, Inc. for its grant support.

Last but by no means least, I want to thank Dean Rusk. Without his enthusiasm and insight, none of this would have been possible. I am proud to call him colleague and friend.

Dorinda G. Dallmeyer

PART ONE

American Attitudes Toward Strategic Defense

1

An Overview of the Strategic Defense Initiative

James A. Abrahamson

It is imperative that the very complex and very difficult discussion of strategic defense should not be conducted at the level of "Star Wars." Star Wars is not the administration's name for the program at all. It has been hooked on the program primarily by the critics of the program. It is not about war, and it is certainly not exclusively about putting weapons in space. Those are all very different.

I do like to point out from time to time, however, that there are some similarities to the movie. In the movie the good guys won and the good guys won primarily because of a force, a mysterious force. In this country this mysterious force is now thousands of dedicated men and women who are working on all aspects of this program, debating the politics, the strategy, and the arms control implications of such a thing. But an even larger number are acting on and working to make the technology a reality so that a new strategy can really become a practical thing for the future.

To provide an overview of the program is an extremely difficult process. I will only be able to touch on a few highlights that I think are very critical. It is best to go back to the president's speech. In that speech when he challenged all of us, "Isn't it better to save lives than avenge them?", he was not talking about weapons in space or weapons of any kind except the ones that have been considered to be the most dangerous and the most destabilizing weapons. These weapons so overbalance our entire military perspective as we look out over what has been now several decades and unfortunately will probably continue to be many decades of military competition with the Soviet Union in the future. These weapons are nuclear ballistic missiles. He did not talk about Star Wars. What he really was doing was raising the question of whether or not there is a better strategy than the strategy of retaliation.

The strategy of retaliation has been our fundamental strategy. It has not been simple mutual assured destruction. Long ago we abandoned the idea that if we had just a few missiles in our country aimed at the cities of the Soviet Union and they had a few missiles in their country aimed at the cities of the United States the situation of mutual terror would be sufficient in fact to stop any major conflagration and certainly the escalation of a crisis into a nuclear war. That idea was something that I think very quickly passed into oblivion. There were many variations on that theme over time. But where we are presently is a military strategy that calls for the United States to have an offensive nuclear force that is composed not only of missiles but also of cruise missiles and aircraft -- a strategy that could assure that in a second-strike mode, if the Soviets started something, that no matter what they did we would have enough surviving forces that we could go forward and destroy the military targets of the Soviet Union such that they could not achieve a military victory either by what they destroyed in this country and what they would have remaining back at home. That essentially is the same way they target as well.

Tragically that does not mean that we would not have incredible civilian casualties that go along with such a strike. I think we all recognize that. We do not know exactly how terrible that would be. Many of us do not know the full implications of the theory of nuclear winter but that is not the issue. The real issue is what is the best way to prevent that nuclear holocaust from ever starting.

We have had several generations in which this strategy of retaliation has worked or at least appeared to work. In my judgment those generations have not, except for one really difficult time during the Cuban missile crisis, ever reached the point where we were faced with the truly incredibly difficult kind of crisis where we could test to see whether the strategy is working or not. Therefore I believe we can say it seems to have worked, but it has never been fully tested and it does not mean that we have clear solid evidence that this is the best strategy for the decades to come.

The president asked if there was a better strategy and that strategy is a defensive deterrence. Many people misunderstand defensive deterrence. We have talked about a

"shield" over the United States. That is not the right
image or the right way to think about this program. They
have talked about being able to absolutely and perfectly
defend and keep every missile out. The goal the president
has set for us is one that calls for research technologies
that will be as effective as humanly possible in preventing
an all-out or even a partial strike and in preventing nuclear missiles from impacting in the United States or among
our allies. But the real question is whether we can find a
defense and the technologies that would be so effective
that the Russian general -- my counterpart in terms of research and development but, more important, the operational
general in charge of their strategic rocket forces -- would
have to turn to his twelve decision-makers sometime in the
future and say "I cannot guarantee to you that I can
achieve the kind of overwhelming military victory that is
worth the risk because of the defenses that the United
States has been able to create." That is defensive deterrence.

The difference between defensive deterrence and offensive deterrence is an important one. If for some terrible
reason, an irrational act, perhaps people being pushed too
far in a crisis situation, offensive deterrence fails, all
8000 warheads arrive. Everyone of them arrives at the targets in this country and in Europe amongst our allies. Most
of the U.S. warheads arrive in the Soviet Union. In the
space business, we call that "fail-deadly." Whether or not
a strategy of fail-deadly is the best strategy for all decades to come is the real question.

If on the other hand, we are successful in some day
developing the kind of layered defensive system that would
be effective enough as a deterrent that they would never
strike because they could not achieve in a first strike
this guaranteed victory or the cost-benefit ratio for them
is so unfavorable, then you do have a perfect defense. So
if again through some tragic miscalculation or incident,
perhaps even started by a third country or a terrorist, the
difference is with the defensive deterrence you are in a
fail-safe situation, meaning that you could stop perhaps
not all the missiles but you could stop up to the level of
effectiveness to which you have been able to build. There
would certainly be tragic consequences if even one nuclear
bomb arrived. Nonetheless we could limit that to something
that our civilization and our ideals hopefully would survive.

What does this mean in terms of a strategy? First it
would be irresponsible to abandon the ABM Treaty now, to

immediately make a commitment to the development and deployment of this kind of system, because it is a very difficult technical problem. Therefore what we have done is what I believe is a responsible step. We have said we are embarking only on a research program that can and should be accomplished under the provisions of the ABM Treaty. There may be some arguments about the interpretations of the treaty but nonetheless we are working very carefully to ensure that we do that. We are trying to see if we can build through research and prove to what will be a skeptical Congress and a number of generals in the Department of Defense a system which will be effective. This research must provide a layered defense that cannot be easily countered or that has a simple Achilles' heel. In spite of some of the critics' creation in their minds of vulnerabilities, it is worthwhile to carefully examine those because countermeasures are not as simple and as straightforward as some of the critics contend.

Finally it has to meet a very important criterion. It has to be affordable. It does not do any of us any good to have a system that we can put out on the table and say buy this and have this be so incredibly expensive that it will not fit into national priorities and all of our other national problems. Therefore the research is aimed at bringing the costs of the technology down, dealing with countermeasures and how one could stop countermeasures, and what effective defense could be built.

We have not been able to have the amount of money we felt we needed for a prudent program. I can understand decisions that have said that the national priorities have to change. Nonetheless we have been reasonably generously provided with funds to proceed at a very difficult time. With the funds we have had we have made incredible progress, much more than even a technical optimist like myself has expected. You have seen only a very few of some of the things we have done. They are rather simple, they are rather straightforward, but the implications of those tests and the other tests are very dramatic.

We have been trying to run an open program to facilitate this national debate. I believe with reasonable funding, by the early 1990s we will be in a position so that we and our allies can make a decision on whether or not to go forward. I am fairly confident that the creative genius of the technical people in this country coupled with the very difficult task of ensuring that we have a stable and effective transition will allow us to have a safer 1990s and certainly a safer next century.

2

The SDI Program
and National Defense

Sam Nunn

Dean Rusk was quoted in the Washington Post as saying, "Star Wars is a matter of the greatest possible consequence to my grandchildren, and those that come beyond them." I think that that is correct. I think this program does have profound consequences both for the short term and the long term. General Omar Bradley once stated, "Ours is a world of nuclear giants and ethical infants. If we continue to develop our technology without wisdom or prudence, our servant may prove to be our executioner." That statement was made several years ago but I think it has continuing and profound consequences for today and tomorrow and the future.

Let me begin by saying that there are several things General James Abrahamson, director of the Strategic Defense Initiative Organization, has said that I want to agree with and identify with. I would say that if General Abrahamson were the sole spokesman for the Strategic Defense Initiative program in this administration it would be in much better shape on Capitol Hill, we would be in much better shape in Geneva, and there would be a much clearer and more realistic understanding of the program throughout the United States. Unfortunately there are many spokesmen in the administration and on Capitol Hill where there are a lot of so-called experts, so we get many different statements that have nuances, that have differences, and sometimes even direct contradictions. This is not good as we move towards Geneva because if we are confused on Capitol Hill where we watch the program rather carefully and hear a great deal of testimony, then certainly it is hard to convey a clear and precise impression of goals and possibilities in both summit conferences and in Geneva arms control discussions.

Let me just pick out a couple of things General Abrahamson said. First he said how do we prevent nuclear

holocaust from ever starting -- that is the essential question, whether we use defenses or offenses or a combination
thereof. That is the essential question and that is the one
thing that all of us can agree on wherever we come down on
this question. And so I think to say that offenses are good
and defenses are bad or that offenses are bad and defenses
are good is a gross oversimplification. Too many times the
Star Wars debate or the SDI debate has evolved in that different pattern. To start categorizing defenses as moral and
offenses as immoral seems to me falls in that same category. I would state that whatever can prevent a nuclear war
between the United States and the Soviet Union in terms of
deterrence, whether it is defense or offense or a combination, is our goal and preventing that war is indeed moral
in my book.

The second thing the general said was that we should
not look at this program as a shield over the United
States. He made it plain that we are not searching for a
perfect defense or one that will not permit any nuclear
weapons to come through. But contrast that to President
Reagan's March 29th speech where he said:

> This is not and should never be misconstrued as just
> another method of protecting missile silos. We're not
> discussing a concept just to enhance deterrence but
> rather a new kind of deterrence, not just an
> addition to our offensive forces but research to
> determine the feasibility of a comprehensive
> non-nuclear defensive system, a shield that could
> prevent nuclear weapons from reaching their targets.

So the word "shield" has been injected by the highest
source, as they say in Washington, and it has been repeated
over and over. Whatever the meaning is, it conveys an impression that we are indeed building or seeking an impenetrable shield.

General Abrahamson also went forward and said we must
have an affordable system. This is certainly in keeping
with the official administration policy because that policy
has been stated very clearly by Ambassador Paul Nitze, one
of the key people advising the secretary of state. Paul
Nitze in a speech on February 20, 1985, in clarifying many
different aspects of the program, stated:

> New defensive systems must also be cost-effective at
> the margin. That is, it must be cheap enough to add
> additional defensive capability so that the other side

has no incentive to add additional offensive
capability to overcome the defense. If the new
technology cannot meet these standards, we're not
about to deploy them.

I have been to Geneva three times this year in my role as
an arms control observer along with Chairman Ted Stevens
and a bipartisan group. One of the fundamental arguing
points that our negotiators have in Geneva is that we are
indeed embarked upon a cost-effective criterion in terms of
the offensive/defensive strategy. That is to say, we have
been trying mightily to convince the Soviets that it does
them no good to say that if we have defenses, they are going to counter that with additional offenses. Our position
has been that those additional offenses will cost more than
our defenses or we would have never deployed the defenses
to begin with and therefore such an effort by the Soviets
is futile. I have never believed that the Soviets were going to buy that argument, but nevertheless that has been a
strong, underlying, fundamental part of the administration
definition of the Strategic Defense Initiative.
    General Abrahamson has agreed to the definition in the
Nitze speech in questions before our committee. But let me
just give you a recent bit of testimony. On October 31,
1985, in testimony to the Senate Foreign Relations Committee, Senator Kerry of Massachusetts asked the following
question to Secretary Weinberger: "If it turns out that
deploying a comprehensive space shield is more expensive
than the cost to the Soviets of additional offensive forces
to overcome it, would you then change your mind?" Answer by
Secretary of Defense Weinberger: "No sir, I would not because I would think that the additional cost in protecting
peoples' lives and protecting this nation would be far
worth anything it would cost." So much for the cost-effectiveness argument in terms of a cohesive administration
position. In closed testimony Assistant Secretary of
Defense Richard Perle in answer to my questions said very
clearly that he agreed with Secretary Weinberger. So cost-
effectiveness is not part of the Defense Department program. These are the various contradictions that cause a
great deal of consternation in terms of those responsible
for not only helping fund the program but also in terms of
trying to see how this all fits into some rational pattern.
    There are a few points that I think are erroneous im-
pressions. I think that there is an erroneous impresssion
that the whole SDI program, or Star Wars as some call it,
started with the presidential speech on March 23, 1983.

General Abrahamson has made brief reference to that as
something of a starting point. It was a major speech. It
did set forth a major direction from President Reagan but
it was not the beginning of vigorous research in this area.
This research program has been going on since the 1970s. It
was accelerated greatly under both Republican and Democratic administrations, including Ford and Carter, before that
March 23, 1983 speech. I was having a closed hearing the
afternoon of the speech. We had all of the experts from the
various laboratories in the country testifying, and we
asked them over and over again if we needed additional
funding for this program. We wanted to give them all the
money they needed for the research on this program. The
answer over and over again was that this program was on a
prudent course with no additional funding needed. That
background is prevalent in terms of people in Congress who
were present and who have memories.

There is another erroneous impression. There is an
impression that the Strategic Defense Initiative program is
totally non-nuclear. There are important parts of the research program that are indeed nuclear. It is clear that
President Reagan intends for the program to be non-nuclear.
It may very well be and it may end up that way. We hope it
can end up that way but we do have very vigorous programs
going on in the nuclear area. I think it is important to
also recognize that if we decide to go forward with deployment of such a system, the Soviets may decide to go nuclear
themselves in terms of defenses. That is something absent
some serious arms control agreements we cannot control.

There is another erroneous impression that the only
basing pattern will be to have space-based systems. General
Abrahamson has not contributed to that misimpression because he makes it very clear before our committee that it
is an option, a real possibility. But it is also entirely
possible that after the research, the experts may decide a
ground-based defensive system would be more survivable and
therefore more feasible and also possibly more economical.

There is another erroneous impression. I get letters
in the mail frequently from people asking how I can still
support the ABM Treaty because it is detrimental to our
security and it is not supported by President Reagan and
the administration. General Abrahamson made it clear the
administration's avowed policy is to continue the ABM Treaty and that our SDI program will fit within the definition
as we interpret that treaty. The real question is not whether the president will give up SDI at Geneva. I think everyone that follows this process recognizes that you cannot

really ban research, you cannot verify research, and it
would be foolish to enter into agreement with the Soviets
to completely ban research because we could not verify whether they complied with such an agreement. So I do not
think research is on the table but clearly our negotiators,
including Max Kampelman, over and over again have said both
offense and defense must be discussed in Geneva. In fact
General Abrahamson has gone over and presented a detailed
explanation to the Soviet negotiators. Those things are
being discussed and to categorize the debate as giving up
SDI in Geneva or keeping it is not only a simplification,
it is an erroneous impression.

Let me just give you briefly my own view. I do not
subscribe to the definition that the president has set
forth. He has strongly insinuated that what we are building
is a population shield. He has also said that our goal is
to render nuclear weapons obsolete. President Carter also
said that. It is a noble goal but in my opinion it is not
directly related to SDI. To give the impression that that
goal is the goal of SDI is an erroneous impression.

Finally the president says that when we get "it", as
if it is in some small package, we are going to turn it
over to the Soviet Union. I do not agree with any part of
that definition. I have supported before the president's
speech, and I continue to support today, a very vigorous
and a very strong research program in this high-technology
area. I think it is enormously important for several reasons. One is to prevent a Soviet breakout or breakthrough
in an important technology that in all likelihood will find
application not only in defensive systems but also in offensive systems, not only in nuclear weapons but also in
conventional weapons. That is a fundamental reason and that
alone justifies a very vigorous research program. Second,
if we do not find a way through either force deployments or
arms control agreements or some combination thereof to reduce the threat of a first strike by the Soviet Union (a
highly unstable situation), I think we may very well need
to have a defensive deployment at some point in the future.
I believe in all logic we should pursue a combination of
arms control and offensive deployment before we make a decision on defensive deployment, but nevertheless a vigorous
program to have ourselves in a position to move in that
direction if required is absolutely essential.

Last but not least, I think the vigorous SDI research
which is now underway is a very important leverage over the
Soviet Union in terms of enticing them to be interested not
only in defensive arrangements, not only in tightening the

ABM Treaty and clarifying definitions, but also most importantly in giving them an incentive to really begin to carry
out the original spirit of the ABM Treaty. That spirit is
that we limit our defenses only on the condition that we
also restrain ourselves with offenses.

It is essential that this debate be clearly understood. I think it would be a great tragedy if the American
people were convinced that what we are building is purely a
shield over the United States and if they believed, as the
television advertisements implied, that the shield would be
impenetrable. One of these days down the road, perhaps under another president, some president of the United States
may very well have to go to the Congress and the American
people and request billions of dollars to be able to protect our ability to survive and retaliate. That means a
protection of perhaps missile fields or bomber bases or
submarine bases. What are people going to believe in Perry,
Georgia, and Peoria, Illinois, and New York City if for
several years they have been bombarded with rhetoric and
television advertisements that basically imply that this
system is going to protect their gardens and their homes?
It is going to be a very severe political reaction. Right
now that kind of rhetoric is very popular but, in my view,
it is also irresponsible.

Discussion

Question: It seems to me that Senator Nunn's skeptical remarks about certain features of the SDI and perhaps also the general's remarks overlook the single most important factor which is often left undiscussed in these forums. That is the absolute necessity left the United States, given Soviet actions which are well on their way toward developing a warfighting-warwinning thermonuclear capability.

In the laundry list of his attorney's nitpicking I think there was a single question raised by Senator Nunn which is substantive. That is the question of cost-effectiveness. But the real question of cost-effectiveness assumes static, unchanging elements of cost and price and benefits and technology. If the history of military technology, especially of crash programs going back to gunpowder and the cannon but especially with reference to the Manhattan Project and also the relevant experience of the NASA program, teaches anything it's that such intensive efforts at the frontiers of science absolutely change the parameters and cause us to redefine the parameters we are dealing with.

In that regard for us not to proceed at the optimal rate -- and I would like to ask General Abrahamson in the context of this what he thinks the program could usefully absorb in terms of research efforts, a dollar figure -- in that context this country has no choice under these circumstances but to most vigorously pursue that end, even if it appears that the single most likely candidate technology might be outstripped in the next cycle of arms competition by the Soviets.

General Abrahamson: The very straightforward answer to the economic part of the question in terms of fiscal year 1986

13

is that our judgment was that we needed approximately 3.7 billion dollars. That was a carefully and, I can assure you, a hard-fought argument between the needs of the Strategic Defense Initiative and the other parts of the defense program and obviously put within the context of what we expected was to be a reasonable defense allocation amongst the total budget priorities of the United States. It appears that we are losing about a billion dollars of that program or about one-fourth of the program.

Now there are two costs whenever that happens. The first cost is the direct cost of certain parts of the technology, certain parts of well-laid plans that have to be put in the backseat or curtailed or stopped. The second one is less obvious but nonetheless very critical. When you lay out a program you lay out one to which you have attracted the best minds in the country. They are expecting that they are going to be able to pursue a particular objective and then each year that has to be scaled back and modified. After a short period of time, these brilliant people just will not tolerate having their experimental goals and their research activities changed and yanked around. We lose some of the best minds.

It is about a billion dollars that we're losing. By the same token, even in this difficult time, it appears that we will nearly double the budget from fiscal 1985 to 1986.

Senator Nunn: Let me just offer a very brief answer. I do not have any real feel for the precise number of dollars needed in this program. The request was 3.75 billion, we had all sorts of proposals to go to 2.0 or 2.5 billion. The Armed Services Committee in the Senate ended up virtually unanimously with a 2.75 billion dollar figure. It looks like that's where the final funding is going to end up. As the program becomes more precise, I think the funding levels will be easier to measure. I believe one of General Abrahamson's top people the other day said that until we have the architecture better defined, we're really flying blind. I think that is true right now. I think we have to move a little bit further along to be able to really precisely measure.

Let me just mention another thing. I certainly agree that the Soviets have moved forward vigorously and they have moved forward without staying in the keeping of the spirit of the ABM Treaty by a very vigorous offensive buildup. Unless that offensive buildup is cut back, unless the president is successful in Geneva, and unless we have a

dramatic reduction of the Soviet's first-strike building
effort, then it seems to me we have to have an option for
defenses. I don't disagree with that at all. I think that
is a key part of why we need SDI.

That is still a far cry from a comprehensive, popula-
tion-protecting type approach. Actually, if you give the
Soviets seven or eight years' notice and tell them you're
going to have a comprehensive shield, even if it works scientifically (which is in some doubt), you would still have
very grave threats to the population of this country
through possible biological warfare, through possible chemical warfare. As a matter of fact, if we can't keep tons of
marijuana from being smuggled across the border, how are we
going to prevent suitcase bombs from being put in somebody's basement? That's a tough thing for an open society.
We have millions of illegal immigrants coming across every
day and we seemingly can't stop that. We haven't been able
to stop massive importation of drugs. You can put a nuclear
weapon in a suitcase now. Within ten or fifteen years it
will probably be much more miniaturized than that, so we
have a number of ways a determined superpower, if they're
willing to suffer grievous damage themselves, can cause
massive population destruction. I don't believe that we're
going to be able to put all those genies back in the bottle. I think SDI has to be measured in that context.

I also believe that you have to measure the Strategic
Defense Initiative along with other defense needs. I would
hate to be in a position by the year 2000 that we had spent
so much on nuclear weapons, so much on strategic defense,
that we didn't have the capability of invading Grenada.

Question: Assuming the fact that SDI could be realized and
that the Soviets could not establish an appropriate coun-
terdefense system, don't you recognize the risk that such a
constellation of defenses would perhaps provoke the Soviets
to stage a nuclear attack?

General Abrahamson: Obviously the key to any scenario of
that kind is the very careful way in which you must coor-
dinate three separate activities. One is the arms control
negotiations effort. Of course we have started that now. We
have tried to discuss with them a stable way so that you
can proceed down a transition from all offense to lesser
degrees of offense and at the same time trying to build up
more and more defense. Deterrence is the sum of those two.
We believe that crisis stability, particularly this first-
strike problem, can be enhanced particularly as you build

up the defensive capability. You do not want to give them
one of these situations so that at 11:59 on June 30, 1999
you have no defense and at 12 noon suddenly it will all be
in place. That's impossible. That's not going to happen.
But you don't want to give them one of those situations
where they will say they must strike. If our present offensive deterrence works at all, it will be enhanced as you
add defenses.

And if our negotiators are successful, and as we do
what the president was driving at, we begin to reduce the
nuclear ballistic missile from its omnipotent status, which
is what it is right now. It is so far out of balance in
terms of its value when you compare it to an airplane in
Europe, when you compare it to a battleship, or any other
thing. Its value in terms of being able to intimidate a
society or to destroy the society afterwards is so incredibly out of balance. That is what the president really
meant when he said can't we make nuclear ballistic missiles
impotent and obsolete, to restore the balance and take them
away. So you try to reduce the value by making them so that
they can be stopped and are not this omnipotent weapon. You
do that gradually. That's why we're negotiating with them
now. I believe that is the kind of scenario that critics
will often raise. I believe that it is a legitimate question to ask. But I don't believe that it is an impossible
kind of a situation to work through.

Senator Nunn: I would not disagree with that answer. I
think on the limited question of Soviet first strike, that
is the way we have to proceed. There is a danger there but
I think the greater danger is the Soviets will greatly proliferate their offensive weapons in response to our defensive systems. That's why cost-effectiveness becomes important. Obviously if they can put in more offensive weapons
than we can put in defenses to cope with them, then what
we're doing is running on a rug. We're spending huge a-
mounts of money, they're spending huge amounts of money,
we're building defenses, they're building offenses.

That's really the way the bomber-penetrating de-
fense/offense battle has gone for years. It's not that we
don't have some precedent. We have years and years of
Soviet Union and other countries (we did it for awhile)
trying to build air defenses. Every time air defenses are
built, the U.S. Air Force has done a darn good job of being
able to overwhelm those defenses. We've got that battle
continuing to run. The B-1 is the latest addition to our
penetrating capability. That's to counter Soviet offenses.

The Stealth bomber program if it comes into fruition, and I'm one of the biggest supporters of that, is going to outmode in our opinion most of the Soviet air defenses. So this is not something that we haven't seen in history. We have had offensive/defensive kinds of races before and we have a continuing one with the bomber situation.

Question: If the funding before the president's speech was at adequate levels according to whoever was doing the research, why has there been the big push in Congress after the president's speech? The second question is whether the ICBM is seeing its last years as the major nuclear force. Aren't we going more to submarine-launched cruise missiles, air-launched cruise missiles, and smaller missiles that really would totally infiltrate any kind of defense system?

Senator Nunn: On the congressional reaction to the president's speech, the Congress has reacted to the speech in a positive way but they haven't bought the whole loaf. That's the reason the 3.7 billion dollar request has been whittled down to about 2.75 billion. There are others who want to go much lower. Actually if you look at the funding level before the president's speech, it was somewhere around 1.5 billion and last year it was around 2.3 billion. So it has grown. I think any time you have that much emphasis on a program, it is going to grow. The question is whether the growth is prudent, cost-effective, and well-managed. All of us wanted and have wanted before the president's speech to give whichever administration was in power all the money they needed for a very vigorous research program in this area. But we don't simply want to throw money at a problem. It's question of trying to give them enough money and when the president says he needs more, obviously that affects the Congress.

General Abrahamson: Let me try to be as accurate as I can about the history of the funding. After the signing of the ABM Treaty, we abandoned our single site defense up in North Dakota. That would have cost a great deal in terms of operational funding to keep that going. There were also some questions about its technical effectiveness and certainly there was a clear understanding that it was a token kind of defense so we gave that up. After that period of time the United States Army continued some investment in the more standard kind of technologies, interceptors with nuclear ballistic missiles which would go up and intercept a nuclear warhead on the way in and different concepts for that. That funding went up and down over the years but essentially was always less than approximately half a billion dollars. There was a lot of additional kind of research in many areas that had some secondary application to the stopping of ballistic missiles. But we in the military departments had accepted the premise that we were not going to in fact try to embark on a vigorous antiballistic missile program. We were just doing minimal kinds of defense work.

It took the president's speech and the challenge to this fundamental acceptance of the idea, to say yes, let's go in and go into more detail. The actual funding in fiscal 1984 that was considered to have some application to this problem was about 950 million dollars in the Department of Defense and about 200 million in the Department of Energy. So you can see that the funding was there but much of that was not specifically aimed at this one goal. What the president's speech did was like what President Kennedy did. He just threw a goal out there and said let's see if we can find the technical means to support this different strategy. That meant that we had to reorient several of these programs. Further we had to add and to make these efforts more robust. And that's why the dollars are going up rather dramatically. Many of these programs do have applications that go well beyond ballistic missile defense. They will affect every other part of our national security forces in some way or another. Furthermore some of them will have commercial applications.

Senator Nunn: Let me just say on that point I agree with that and that's why we need to look very skeptically at any statement that we're going to turn over this technology to the Soviet Union.

General Abrahamson: As far as the usefulness of ICBMs is concerned, the United States started moving away from ballistic missiles into cruise missiles because we felt that we wanted to have something that would have more stability in terms of something that would get there slower and would be a survivable retaliatory kind of strike. The Soviet Union was doing the same and our total strategic retaliatory force was coming more and more in question. I talked about two or three factors that were the long-term trends that the president was concerned about. One was the inability to stop the growth of nuclear ballistic missiles and their warheads and their deliverable megatonnage on the part of the Soviet Union. The Soviets continued to do research in defense as well. The Krasnoyarsk radar, which is

clearly a violation of the ABM Treaty, had to have been in
planning either at the time of the negotiations or perhaps
a few years afterwards, including its location. That is not
something that seems to have sprung full-blown since the
president's speech or in reaction to the president's
speech.

Would the nuclear ballistic missile die out of its
own? I think not because it is so effective as a first-
strike and as an intimidation weapon. With defenses I think
it can.

Question: Senator, the reason for my question is that you
are described in Forbes Magazine as every Democratic presidential candidate's choice for vice-president in 1988. My
question is, if you were to shift to the executive branch
of government, what changes if any would you like to see in
the direction this program is taking?

Senator Nunn: I haven't caught that vice-presidential or
presidential fever. It's nice to be mentioned in that vein
but I'm not pursuing that goal. I would say that I would
start with the definition. I would not say that the goal of
this is to abolish nuclear weapons from the earth. That
goal is going to require a moral and ethical and philosoph-
ical dimension that the SDI program cannot touch. And that
goal is many years away. I think when you discuss that goal
it ought to be discussed in those terms rather than believing that we can use technology to put technology back in
the bottle. I don't think that is going to happen.

Second, I do not believe that we ought to say that
we're going to turn this over to the Soviets. This is either going to be believed and accepted or it's not going to
be believed and scoffed at. There's very little in between.
It seems to me, as General Abrahamson said, you don't just
build defensive technology. You have all sorts of fallout,
offensive-type fallout. I would like to see as one of the
fundamental things I hope comes out of this program, even
if by accident, an infantry-capable weapon to kill tanks. I
think if you could kill Soviet tanks with a handheld weapon
from concealed places with infantry it would have as much
to do with the balance of power in the world, maybe even
more, than an attempted effort to build a shield. So I
would change the definition.

By changing the definition I would then channel brilliant people like General Abrahamson and the team he's gotten together and the people here at Georgia Tech that are
brilliant into a realistic goal that can be achieved. In my

opinion it could be sustained politically if it's realistic
and unless it's sustained politically, we will not have the
kind of continuing leverage we need with the Soviets. So
I'd change the definition.

General Abrahamson: I do need to make some important clarifying points, Senator. By the way, we appreciate all the
points and I'm taking some very careful notes in case after
1988 in fact you are in a position to change the program.
All of us want this to be a national program, nationally
supported on a bipartisan basis. The question is not can we
do something technically. We can. We have incredible technical muscle in this country. We can do whatever this nation really does have the will and the judgment and the
wisdom to say we must do. I truly believe that.
     But notice I put a technical limit on that. The use of
the word "shield" and our difficulty explaining this led me
in 1984 to despair when the press as well as the politicians on all sides who dealt with this program reduced it
to what I call bumpersticker logic. This is complex business. We're not even beginning to get down to the depths of
the arguments here. There is lots of time and effort and
deep intellectual thought that has to be put into it. In
the early days when it was described as "war in the hea-
vens" or "peace on earth" with that bumpersticker logic,
one of our congressmen put it very well. He said "You engage in bumpersticker logic and you get government by t-
shirt." That is indeed what is not good.
     It has been many of our critics of the program who
have either forced us or who have promulgated these sim-
plistic methods of describing the program. The Union of
Concerned Scientists, who I am sure is a group of very sin-
cere people who have opposed the program, introduced the
phraseology "an astrodome over the United States." That is
not at all what we are trying to do. I'm sure that they
didn't do it in any way except to try to find simple and
easy ways to describe it, just as the term "shield" has
gotten introduced in a oversimplistic way. I do believe
that there is no misunderstanding on the part of the president, the secretary of defense, and on my part that our
goal is a long-term goal, as I said earlier, to see if we
can find the technology which would be implementable in an
affordable way to make a capability, a defense of the kind
that it could first of all deter against a first strike and
in that sense be perfect, but second of all, be as effective as humanly possible.

We need tough goals and in that sense we have been
given tough goals. To the extent that these have been badly
used in some cases by the press and in many cases by over-
enthusiastic supporters and in some cases by oversimplistic
critics, I decry that and I feel bad about that. I think
the American people are capable of understanding these
things. While I have criticized the press and some of our
people in 1984 I am now getting to be much more encouraged
because what I see is people spending much more time, the
television media spending in-depth efforts trying to understand this, the press going through series of articles,
usually more balanced. I'm a Jeffersonian kind of American,
not a Hamiltonian kind of American. I believe our people
can make good solid judgments. But they do have to have
facts laid out well.

We have to have goals, demanding goals, and that is
why we have have been given that. I am encouraged now as
the press and others look for these more in-depth discussions because then as we make progress, and as that progress can be measured for not only its near-term implications but the long-term implications, it will start a defense that will improve and improve over decades and hopefully at the same time reduce offensive weapons. Just think
of the marvelous combination of a reduction in offensive
weapons by half and what that does to any level of effectiveness of a defensive system someday that you might have.
It increases it dramatically. Once we can start this cycle,
and that's the real issue, if we can start the cycle, moving down in offensive weapons and improving defense, who
knows where that final goal can lead? And that is certainly
I think a hope that we should all have. But it should be,
as the Senator and many of us all believe, a realistic hope
and it should be combined with realistic plans to get
there.

PART TWO

Technical and Scientific Issues

3

SDI: Technical Reality and Political Intransigence

Daniel O. Graham

It is my view that SDI is not a technical problem but political problem. It is a matter of whether we have the will to change a strategy. SDI after all is not a weapons program and it should not be just a research program. SDI is in fact a change of strategy. When the president announced his determination to go this direction, he said essentially that he was tired of the old mutual assured destruction construct and he would like to have our deterrent based on non-nuclear defense instead of nuclear offense. That is what he was talking about when he said wouldn't it be better to save lives than to avenge them. It is that strategy change which is the matter that has to be decided and it is not a matter of whether there is enough technology around to make that strategy change.

You hear a lot of scientists who say they are against SDI. Many of them are nuclear scientists, but nuclear technology has very little to do with SDI. Who you need to listen to are men in the right fields, like astrophysicists. I do not know what the count would actually be if you could count the scientists and engineers who do not make statements for television and the press. My guess is that for every scientist that is sounding off against this issue, there are probably ten working on it. To believe that, all you have to do is go to the SDI office and see all the proposals for research. You realize then that there is an enormous number of scientists who want to be part of SDI and are not out to say it is impossible.

When people start talking about technology you need to make one judgment, either from what the person has said previously or by listening to his arguments as he sounds off. Many of the people who are talking about the technical difficulties of a strategic defense are people who would

not put up a strategic defense if it did not cost us a
nickel and we could do it tomorrow. Therefore their judgments on technology result from a diligent search for
"showstoppers", i.e., to try to find reasons to say it will
not work.

We have some good evidence around that SDI will work.
We got a good piece of evidence on June 10, 1984, when we
shot a warhead down 120 miles up in space and we did not
even use any exotic technology like lasers. We shot a warhead down with direct impact from a kinetic-energy kill
system. This system has always been the favorite of my organization, High Frontier. Kinetic-energy kill systems are
basically off-the-shelf, straightforward technology that
could be put up on enough satellites to cover the Soviet
Union. This basic system is rarely talked about because it
is a lot easier to dazzle people by talking about lasers
and particle beam weapons. The average person's eyes glaze
over unless they are really into directed energy weapons.
We have always maintained that we can do quite well with a
kinetic defense system.

In order to have a workable kinetic-energy system,
you first have to be able to detect the fact that a lot of
missiles have been fired and that the defensive system must
be put into operation. We already have that system. I even
helped put that into space when I was deputy director of
the Central Intelligence Agency. This system makes 1.2 billion computations per second. It detects missile launches
by the glare emitted by a long-range ballistic missile, a
glare so bright that the only naturally-occurring phenome-
non that compares with it is the sun itself.

The next requirement is that you be able to track that
strong signature as it moves up through the atmosphere and
into space and determine what its trajectory through space
will be. We can already do that, although we cannot yet
track it well enough to put a pencil beam of laser light on
it, track it around, and kill it. That is a serious technical problem. But if instead you fire a cloud of pellets
400 feet in diameter and 4000 feet long at it, the tracking
problem is essentially solved.

Next you have to contend with the problem that if you
do not get the missile in the first nine minutes of trajectory when everything is clustered very close together, you
may begin to get a cloud of decoys and warheads in space
that gets bigger and bigger. The question then is whether
one must track every object in that cloud. If you want to
have a perfect system you would. But if you want to have a
system where the Soviets have no confidence in firing a

first strike, you don't. You just take down everything that
comes and if you use a large cloud of kinetic-energy pellets then you just fire into the middle of the enemy cloud
and get everything you can. Quite likely, if you fire in
the middle you will get the warheads because they are heav-
ier and they do not spread out the way light decoys will
spread out. There are even fancy ways of doing it like ap-
plying some light to the decoys and the light itself will
slow them down more than the warheads. So discrimination is
not an insurmountable problem.

Finally, command and control seems to be the last
ditch of the naysayers who say SDI cannot be done because
the computers will not handle it. Some have said that SDI
will require computer systems that have several million
lines of software. It took seven million lines of software
for the shuttle program and took fifty million lines for
AT&T's telephone switching system. Obviously the computer
work is not an impossible thing to do.

If this is not a technical impossibility then how can
legitimate technical people claim otherwise? It is very
easy as long as you preface your statements with the words
"In order to get a perfect or leakproof defense...." Then
you can defeat this whole idea in two paragraphs because
man does not make things that are perfect. Furthermore you
can extrapolate enormous costs because anybody who has
dealt in a technical field knows that when you try to get
something from very good, say 95 percent effective, to 100
percent effective that is where all the costs and technical
difficulty come in. I do not care whether you are trying to
make a perfect ball bearing or a perfect defense system. So
you will hear, time and time again, the preamble to the
technical argument to be "In order to get a perfect defense...." Of course it then follows that with that very
vulnerable strawman set up it is a piece of cake to tear it
down.

Where do we get the notion that what we are after is
perfection? You get it from two sources. The president, in
a flight of political rhetoric that I wish he had not used,
said that he wanted to make nuclear weapons impotent and
obsolete. That is a nice thought but it was not a program
description. This was not a specification for the program
to be pursued. But it has been used as such by the naysayers who want to paint a problem that is so difficult you
cannot solve it. Then we had tremendous opposition in the
Pentagon to going this direction. So those of you who might
believe that this is a great plot of the Pentagon to seize
space technology should think again. The Pentagon was

behaving the way the cavalry generals did back in the early
1900s when somebody suggested that the airplane could be
used for some distinct advantage. Those generals said only
that it might be useful for delivering messages and doing
reconnaissance but not for any real military use. The cavalry generals did everything they could to prevent the use
of aircraft in the military forces. Now we have the same
syndrome going on in the Pentagon today. They want to use
space for what they have been using it for, i.e, as support
for mutual assured destruction strategy. When the president
said he did not want that anymore, then suddenly their programs were in danger. There was tremendous opposition within the Pentagon for going this direction. Unfortunately
there still is some although most of them are falling in
behind their commander-in-chief who has told them what he
wants the strategy to be. There is still that resistance
and it was very strong when this idea was broached.

When Dr. James Fletcher was given the charge of seeing
what technology was available to do what the president
wanted, lo and behold he got a description of what he was
to aim for, which was a 99.99 percent effective defense.
Those of you who have worked on technical problems know
that this is what is called "spec-ing it to death," that
is, putting specifications out that destroy the whole idea
and that is what a lot of people in the Pentagon were trying to do with this system. They said that they wanted to
get rid of this idea and get rid of it quick because it was
going to endanger programs for more offensive systems and
cause us to put money where we had not intended to put it.
These people like the bureaucratic rut they are in and they
wanted to stay in it.

They were supported by people who have been pursuing
arms control under the old concept of mutual assured destruction. We have been pursuing arms control to try to
create some kind of balance within the balance of terror.
If you go toward strategic defense you have to start negotiating for mutual assured survival instead of negotiating
for the balance of terror that will support mutual assured
destruction. So the Pentagon naysayers got some support
from the arms control naysayers and the State Department
naysayers. They came out with this attempt to kill the
thing with the specification of 99.99 percent effective.
Dr. James Fletcher recognized that they were proposing
something that makes SDI an extremely academic exercise
where we have to be looking way out in the future to super-
exotic systems trying to get that measure of perfection. He
finally talked them into lowering the percentage by 0.09 to

99.9 percent. Yet he still concluded, along with most of
the scientists on the Fletcher Commission, that even that
level of effectiveness could be achieved. He had to force
on the Pentagon an examination by his commission of the
near-term solutions which of course are not 99.9 percent
effective.

If you look at the SDI effort in the proper light,
which is not as an attempt to make the United States incap-
able of being struck by a nuclear weapon but as a system
which will drive the possibility of nuclear war as close to
zero as possible (and I want a system that takes care of
accidental strike by long-range ballistic missile, which
nobody else's proposition has take care of), then how good
does it have to be? It doesn't have to be as good as many
experts say it can be. i.e., 90 to 95 percent effective.
Why is this lower level effective? Because 90 to 95 percent
effective gives 100 percent protection to the entire country. No Soviet marshal is ever going to fire those weapons
with a five to ten percent possibility of success. He is
not going to do it. The Soviets do not have 6000 warheads
sitting over there on weapons because they want to dump
them in the middle of the United States. They have specific
targets for them and even if you could take out just 50
percent of them, you would drive the possibility of nuclear
war a lot closer to zero than it is today. If you can take
out 90 percent you literally drive it to the point of zero.
This is why you should have SDI.

Furthermore, you should have SDI to guard against what
some mathematicians say is an absolute certainty that one
day some long-range nuclear-tipped ballistic missile will
in fact be fired by accident. Should we remain totally
naked to attack so that all the president can do is call up
the city involved and say, "I'm sorry to tell you this,
mayor, but you're about to lose a million people." Is that
what we want? Do we want to stay in this crazy situation of
nuclear terror? Is that what we should leave to our children and grandchildren? Even if some naysayers would agree
that is a bad idea, they would say that we should turn to
the diplomats to handle it by making some kind of a deal
with the Soviet Union. I cannot say that that is totally
impossible nor should they say that defense is totally impossible. But if you look at the record of American
achievement and what kind of Americans really do good work,
I bet on the engineers and not the diplomats. That is not
biased. The record of American engineering is brilliant
while the record of American diplomacy is dismal. If you
are going to bet your future, the future of your children

and grandchildren, the future of this great nation, the
future of our allies all around the world on our diplomats,
I think it is a pretty weak bet.

Furthermore, if we go this direction we will continue
to see what we have already started to see as a result of
this effort, that the Soviets suddenly become rather interested in actual reduction of nuclear weapons. We should
never trade off SDI for any mess of potage from the Soviet
Union. We must pursue it and must not allow technical ob-
jection based on the notion that it is no good unless it is
perfect to stand in our way. With SDI, five percent will
get through if deterrence breaks down; if deterrence breaks
down today, all of them get through. Try to make the argument to the ordinary man in the street that we are just as
bad off being hit by 300 hundred warheads as by 6000. He
will not buy that because he is too bright. It takes a defense intellectual to wrap his mind around the notion that
this country is as bad off by being hit by 300 weapons as
by 6000.

Will it save people if it is imperfect? Of course it
will. If we take any city at random in the United States,
say Ithaca, New York, then how many of the 6000 weapons on
the Soviet long-range ballistic missiles do you think are
aimed at Ithaca? That probably has something to do with
your civic pride as to how important the Soviets think Ithaca is and how mad they are at it. If they want to attack
Ithaca, they do not have to put more than three warheads in
their target plan. If we can stop 95 percent of those weapons, the chances of the three aimed at Ithaca being in the
five percent that get through are pretty low. You do not
have to be Mr. Einstein to figure that one out. So are you
protecting the people of Ithaca with SDI? You bet you are.
Are you protecting the people who might be around a military target? You bet you are. We are not talking about an
SDI system that reads a sign on the side of the missile
that indicates whether it is headed for a silo or a city
but a system that takes out the missiles as they come up
and coast through space and as they hit the ground.

For those of my fellow American citizens who buy the
Soviet view that somehow this represents the militarization
of space, I say step back a minute. What militarizes space?
The most awesome space weapon today is the long-range ballistic missile that the SDI is designed to defeat. The
long-range ballistic missile spends a few minutes on earth
and then it goes through space to do its dirty business.
Not to include these ICBMs that SDI is to defend against as
space weapons is like referring to a battleship as not a

naval weapon because it happens to be in port. Space is already militarized and not just with our reconnaissance satellites. Space was militarized with the long-range ballistic missile. SDI is designed to get rid of that militarization of space with non-nuclear defensive systems.

4

Technical Impediments to a Workable Defense System

Kosta Tsipis

On March 23, 1983, President Reagan called upon the scientific community to give this country the means to render nuclear weapons "impotent and obsolete." Six days later, in remarks at the National Space Club, Mr. Reagan further explained, "We are not discussing a concept just to enhance deterrence, not just an addition to our offensive forces, but research to determine the possibility of a nonnuclear defense system -- a shield that could prevent nuclear weapons from reaching their targets."

I take this to mean that whatever the system envisioned by the president, it must be able to intercept all nuclear weapons aimed at the United States since even if a few reach their urban targets, we would suffer tens of millions of dead and wounded and the loss of cities worth hundreds of billions of dollars to weapons that cost just a few million dollars each. The Strategic Defense Initiative Organization, established to implement Mr. Reagan's plan, aims at developing systems to counter only ballistic missiles. No provisions are foreseen for defense against bombers and cruise missiles that could deliver nuclear weapons against U.S. targets or against clandestine introduction of nuclear explosives on ships or even trucks or cars into this country as do thousands of tons of narcotics every year. Therefore, even if the Strategic Defense Initiative were completely successful, the country would still remain woefully vulnerable to nuclear attack.

A more realistic goal which, however, contradicts Mr. Reagan's call for a perfect defense, is promoted in papers issued by the White House and by General James Abrahamson. On October 25, 1984, the general said in a speech, "So for the technical viewpoint, we are pursuing this program to increase deterrence and stability." A White House paper on

SDI issued in January 1985 avers that "The purpose of SDI
is to identify ways to exploit recent advances in ballistic
missile defense technologies that have potential for
strengthening deterrence." What strengthens deterrence is
not clear to me. But in April 1983, the president's own
commission on strategic forces known as the Scowcroft Commission concluded in its report, "The Commission believes
that no antiballistic missile defense technologies appear
to combine practicality, survivability, low cost, and technical effectiveness sufficiently to justify proceeding beyond the stage of technology development." An even more
pessimistic view was struck Dr. Richard DeLauer, who at
that time was undersecretary of defense for research and
engineering, who said in July 1983, "There is no way an
enemy cannot overwhelm your defenses if he wants to badly
enough. It makes a lot of difference in what we do if we
have to defend against a thousand reentry vehicles or ten
thousand of them."

These statements which go from one end of the spectrum
to the other are terribly confusing. In this paper I will
try to bring to bear on these conflicting views whatever
general considerations physics and common sense afford us
in order to decide which of the above statements will prove
to come closest to the pragmatic truth in the years to
come.

A ballistic missile that carries tens of reentry vehicles and hundreds of decoys takes about thirty minutes to
cover the distance from the Soviet Union to the United
States. For current missiles the boost phase, during which
the missile is accelerated to its terminal required veloci-
ty, lasts about 200 seconds. The technology exists now to
build missiles that can complete their boost in fifty seconds while still inside the atmosphere. At the end of the
boost, the MIRV bus begins releasing the individual reentry
vehicles and accompanying decoys, a process that can last a
few minutes. Each reentry vehicle and decoy coasts in the
vacuum of outer space unpowered for about twenty minutes,
influenced only by the local gravitational field, in an
elliptical trajectory that takes it to an apogee of about a
thousand kilometers above the earth. Finally, each reentry
vehicle crashes back into the atmosphere at about seven
kilometers per second where it is violently decelerated and
overheated by friction with the air molecules. For that
reason, reentry vehicles are made to resist temperatures of
2000 to 3000 degrees Fahrenheit and extreme mechanical
stresses. Reentry, effectively starting at about a hundred
kilometers above the surface of the earth, lasts another

five minutes or so until the reentry vehicle reaches its target.

The Strategic Defense Initiative planners have proposed to erect several different defense barriers against such a weapon. First comes the boost-phase defense system that would detect and attack the missile itself during its boost phase as it rises from its silo. Then a second midcourse system would distinguish reentry vehicles from decoys and attack the individual reentry vehicles during their coasting. Finally there would be a third terminal defensive system that would detect any deceptive reentry vehicles during their passage through the atmosphere on their way to the targets. If the reentry vehicles were aimed against cities, interceptions would have to occur at about 10,000 to 20,000 feet. If silos were the targets of the reentry vehicles, interception is possible almost all the way to the ground.

The boost-phase defensive system is considered the most important, but also the easiest, component of the defense. The boosting missile can be detected with relative ease because of the large infrared signature of its exhaust plume. Its structure is relatively fragile and quite large, so it is easier to hit and damage than are the reentry vehicles. It is important to hit the booster because each such missile at the boost phase carries about ten reentry vehicles and hundreds of decoys that can be neutralized all at once if the missile is destroyed.

To attack the booster one must be in sight of it. The easiest approach would be to place a rapid-firing cannon right next to each Soviet silo and fire on the missile as it rises from it. But this system would be assuredly subject to rather effective countermeasures and therefore it is not considered a viable system. Instead there have been proposals to place weapons on satellites in lower earth orbit that could, during a brief portion of their orbit, have Soviet silos in sight. There have been five types of weapons proposed for mounting on the satellites: neutral atomic hydrogen beams; large chemical lasers; kinetic-energy weapons that could fire small masses of 10 to 100 grams, propelled to velocities of several kilometers per second and aimed to hit the rising booster or a different kind of kinetic-energy weapon which fires small self-guided rockets that could be fired from the satellite and guide themselves to hit the booster; nuclear-pumped x-ray lasers, either deployed in orbit or popped up from submarines lurking in the Indian Ocean or the Persian Gulf to altitudes which would permit line-of-sight views of the rising Soviet

ICBMs, to fire intense pulses of soft x-rays generated by
the explosion of a nuclear device; and, a combination of
large mirrors on the ground, transmission mirrors in geosynchronous orbit and smaller mirrors in low-earth orbit
which could direct the laser light that would have arrived
via the transmission mirrors against the rising missile.

Each of these weapons suffers from three classes of
difficulties: intrinsic technical difficulties, countermeasures against them, and operational difficulties. The major
technical difficulty is that none of the proposed systems
exists. There have been demonstrations of the principles of
large chemical lasers but at an order of magnitude smaller
than what the actual weapon would require. It is not known
whether these prototypes can be scaled to the required energy and power levels because lasers are nonlinear systems.
We do not know whether we can just indefinitely expand them
or whether modular assembly, i.e., having many lasers all
in phase attacking the same target, is feasible. The advanced high-energy lasers we possess now do not have the
proper wavelength to be useful as weapons. Lasers with the
right wavelength are at an embryonic state of technical
development billions of times weaker than needed.

Particle beam, laser, and kinetic-energy weapons will
require enormous amounts of energy supplies carried into
orbit. Each lethal shot of laser light or burst of parti-
cles requires about a ton of fuel. Each weapon must be able
to fire several shots at about a thousand missiles. So each
weapon-carrying satellite must carry several thousand tons
of fuel. There has been heated debate on how many such satellites are needed to cover Soviet missile fields at all
times. Calculations vary from 427 to 2263 satellites
depending upon what one assumes about the number of missiles, their basing configuration, their boost time, and
the slew time of the defensive weapons for changing aim
from one missile to the next. The cost per booster kill,
according to these numbers, is somewhere between 700 million and 2.1 billion dollars per missile, depending on missile boost time and the size of the laser mirror, if lasers
were to be used in orbit. The shorter the boost time and
the smaller the mirror, the more expensive each kill becomes. Lasers are the only conceivable boost-phase weapons.
Since a missile costs millions of dollars, the Soviets can
assuredly drive us to the poorhouse by building more of
them or by placing missile dummies on the ground, forcing
us to deploy additional satellites with weapons overhead.

The ground-based laser (clearly cheaper because you do
not have to carry the fuel into space) with two families of

mirrors, one in geosynchronous orbit and one in near-earth orbit, will require transmission mirrors that must be at once very large (at least five meters in diameter if excimer lasers are ever developed to the power we need them), very robust, cooled, incorporating adaptive optics, and capable of fractions of microradian aiming. It is not clear at this time that the properties of materials at hand can support such a mirror system which would be vulnerable to simple Soviet attacks anyway.

Excimer lasers that can be based on the ground are a billion times weaker than what is required and would be useless on a cloudy day. Since the mirrors both in high and low orbits will be defenseless, the opponent can attack and destroy them prior to launching his own nuclear missiles. Since he can attack at will, he can choose a cloudy day in the United States to launch his attack.

Countermeasures are the most serious difficulty faced by the proposed weapons systems. All satellites in orbit can be attacked by the Soviets and destroyed. Dr. Edward Teller, a strong supporter of SDI, on April 4, 1983, said, "The Soviets can get rid of orbiting systems at one-tenth the cost of putting them there." The Fletcher report says, "Survivability of the system components is a critical issue whose resolution requires a combination of technologies and tactics that remain to be worked out." Countermeasures other than direct attack include hardening the missiles, hiding or spoofing their infrared signatures, blinding the sensors and detectors of the orbiting defense weapons, or jamming their communications with their command computers and each other. The electromagnetic pulse from nuclear explosions in space can destroy their electronics as well as the computers that must control them.

In addition, Martin-Marietta, an experienced company in missile construction, has shown that missiles with burn times of fifty seconds are technically feasible now. As a result, the particle beam weapons, the hypervelocity kinetic-energy weapons, and the x-ray laser will be unable to attack Soviet missiles that complete their boost within the atmosphere fifty seconds after launch because the atmosphere will attenuate or disperse their beams and vaporize the kinetic-energy weapon projectile. The other types of weapons -- space-borne chemical lasers or ground-based excimer lasers with orbiting mirrors -- will have only fifty seconds to destroy the ascending wave of a thousand such missiles, increasing the cost of each kill proportionately.

These countermeasures are neither less effective nor less feasible than those the Soviets would apply against

the rapid-fire cannons next to their silos. Yet, while no
one is proposing to install such cannon-based missile defense, the Strategic Defense Initiative office insistently
ignores the inescapable efficacy of countermeasures against
space-based weapons intended to attack Soviet missiles during their boost phase.

Boost phase and midcourse defensive systems designed
to attack either the bus during the MIRVing process or
individual reentry vehicles could be either chemical rockets fired from platforms in near-earth orbit with velocities of a few kilometers per second or hypervelocity electromagnetic guns firing solid pellets at five kilometers
per second or even faster. These systems face two extremely
difficult problems: detecting and tracking their targets
which are now reentry vehicles or decoys, and discriminat-
ing between real warheads inside decoy-like balloons and
thousands of decoys that could accompany the real reentry
vehicles. A reentry vehicle is a hardened object that can
tolerate very large mechanical loads and skin temperatures
up to about 2000 degrees Fahrenheit. After they leave the
missile at the end of the boost phase, they have a very
weak, evanescent infrared signature. Any rocket designed to
home on such a signature must have an infrared sensor
cooled to a few degrees Kelvin. The cooling system will
have to be bulky and heavy. Thus each such rocket would be
expensive and the platforms that carry them would have to
be very large indeed. The weight to be carried into orbit
to form such a defensive system could easily reach many
tens of thousands of tons.

An alternative approach would be to illuminate the
reentry vehicles with a laser based in geosynchronous orbit. Small rockets fitted with light sensors would detect
the laser light reflected from the reentry vehicles and
home onto them. You do not need cooling for that and therefore all that weight penalty goes away. But this scheme
also requires that the real reentry vehicles are recognized
among thousands of decoys. Such defenses can be easily
overcome by accompanying each real reentry vehicle with
many tens of lightweight balloon-like decoys while enclo-
sing each reentry vehicle in a similar balloon, or what we
call antisimulation. You end up with hundreds of thousands
of identical-looking objects during an attack of which ten
thousand will contain real bombs and the rest will be empty
decoys with no way to discriminate between them.

In testimony to the House of Representatives, the
Reagan administration's Undersecretary for Defense for Research and Engineering Richard DeLauer said, "Any defensive

system can be overcome with proliferation and decoys, decoys, decoys." There appears to be no practical way, either
passive or active, to weigh all the identical-looking balloons during their twenty-minute flight to discover which
contain real reentry vehicles and which are empty. Such
decoys can be proliferated at will and at low cost and can
incorporate spoofing features unsuspected by the defense
before the attack begins. There is not even a viable theo-
retical concept at this time for an effective midcourse
defense against such a projected massive threat of tens of
thousands of warheads and perhaps even up to a million decoys.

Additional countermeasures would include attacking the
midcourse defensive platforms in orbit, and increases of
background radiation by high altitude nuclear detonations
that could blind or confuse the sensors of the defense.
There is no new technology on the horizon that could help
alleviate these problems. The fact that the offense, by
altering its tactics or the observables of the reentry vehicles and decoys, can present an entirely unforeseen
threat configuration to the defense exacerbates the already
bleak prospect for an effective midcourse defensive system.

Terminal defenses, in contrast, are not plagued by the
decoy problems since in the atmosphere the decoys will
quickly burn up. Terminal defenses have been helped by recent technological advances in guidance, homing sensors,
very high acceleration rockets, and modular very fast computers. Yet terminal defense of the population, industry,
and soft military targets is bound to be ineffective since
this defensive layer, given the fact that boost-phase and
midcourse defenses do not appear to have any chances of
being effective, will be faced with the threat of thousands
of reentry vehicles descending hidden behind fireballs of
deliberately detonated Soviet nuclear weapons. Only a hand-
ful of these reentry vehicles can destroy an equal number
of targets if they leak through. Since high accuracy is not
required when attacking cities, salvage-fusing and maneu-
vering reentry vehicles can further exacerbate the difficulties of terminal defense of urban and industrial centers
and soft military targets.

All these difficulties, however, are dwarfed by the
operational problems of such a multilayer defensive system.
By the very nature of its mission, such a system can never
be tested or exercised. The tens of millions of lines of
computer code that must support the operation of its massive computational network can never be confidently debug-
ged. The space shuttle program is four million lines and

look at the results. There has never been a space shuttle launched without delays or aborts attributable to computer bugs somewhere. After all these space shuttle launches, still there are bugs in the four million line program. The AT&T program has an entirely different mission. The way AT&T approaches the problem of using computers to route telephone calls is to have a very small test example of the system which they work for years. As they work they find mistakes and as they find mistakes they correct them. And after many years of testing and debugging, then they put the system into operation. That is exactly the opposite of what we have to do in a defensive system where we have to push the button and it has to work the first time you expect it to. The codes can never be tested against the possibility of failure under unforeseen circumstances. Therefore there will always be the probability that at least some computers of the defensive system will grind to a halt. Faced with the unexpected, the system as a whole may probably degrade ungracefully. The myriad of command, control, and communication links several orders of magnitude more extensive and more complex than the command and control of our current defensive weapons could be disrupted in a number of ways by the Soviet Union prior to or during an attack. While the defense has only a half hour to perform its function with little or no prior knowledge of the exact configuration of the threat, the offense can prepare for years, devise secret countermeasures, and choose the moment and the form of attack.

Consider for example what can happen to the algorithms embedded in the software of the defensive system intended to enable the computers to recognize a missile or to discriminate between a decoy and the Real McCoy -- a warhead. These algorithms must be written on the basis of imperfect information regarding the complexion of the threat years before they are called to perform. At the time of the attack, not only would they not have been tested against a realistic threat, but they most probably will be called to perform faced with unexpected threat configurations, changed observables, new decoys, unpredicted background clutter, or radiation. There is no reason to believe that these algorithms will perform at all, let alone 90 to 95 percent effectively as required. It is not possible to simulate a Soviet attack since we will not know how it would look and we could not duplicate the nuclear environment in which it would take place anyway.

Aside from what the Strategic Defense Initiative Organization has been proposing as defensive systems, there has been another effort going on to design, develop, and deploy space-based defenses against ballistic missiles which is only indirectly related to President Reagan's call. It is what is popularly known as the High Frontier proposal, promoted by General Daniel Graham. According to the book, this proposal envisions 456 satellites in low-earth orbit, each carrying a number of self-guided rockets that could attack ascending Soviet ICBMs during their boost phase. This proposal claims that the envisioned defense system could be built with existing off-the-shelf techno-logy and could be fully deployed for ten to fifteen billion dollars. However, the Department of Defense obtained a much higher estimate than that. Shortly after the High Frontier report was published, Dr. Robert Cooper, director of the Defense Advanced Research Projects Agency, commented on the proposal for a subcommittee of the Senate committee on armed services. Dr. Cooper said:

> The Department of Defense has worked with the High Frontier analysts throughout the development of their concept and supports the basic damage-denial goal. However, as hardware developers of warfighting systems, we do not share their optimism in being able to develop and field such a capability within their timeframe and cost projections. We have conducted several in-house analyses and have experienced some difficulties in ratifying the existence of off-the-shelf components or technologies to provide the required surveillance, command and control, and actually perform the intercepts within the orbital and physical conditions described. Our understanding of the system's implications and costs will lead us to project expenditures of the order of 200 billion dollars in acquisition costs alone for the proposed system.

John Gardiner, director of defensive systems in the Pentagon, arrived at similar conclusions about the High Frontier proposal in testimony on March 23, 1983, to the Senate committee on armed services. He said:

> The entire High Frontier proposal is technically unsound. It suffices to mention that it requires the kill rockets that attack the Soviet ICBM to be fired against it 53 seconds before the target ICBM was launched, with no explanation of how the defense would

know 53 seconds in advance when and where the launch
would occur.

In addition, both Dr. Gardiner in his testimony and
General Abrahamson in testimony he gave of February 21,
1985, before a Senate armed services subcommittee empha-
sized the great vulnerability of the High Frontier platforms to simple Soviet attack. As a consequence, the High
Frontier proposal is not a candidate system for further
exploration by the Strategic Defense Initiative office.

Where does that leave us? When we make an engineering
judgment regarding the feasibility of Star Wars defenses,
we must look beyond our capability to manufacture a ten
meter mirror or a 25 megawatt hydrogen fluoride laser. We
must look at the required performance of the entire system
and how its performance will degrade if a systematic error
or flaw appears during its brief operational time. We cannot in good technical judgment consider the system outside
its engagement environment which is going to be both hostile and totally unpredictable. Finally we must consider
not only the cost of erecting such a defensive system but
also the infinitely larger cost if it fails under attack
because if we rely on defenses to avoid the nuclear incin-
eration of our country, there is nothing to save us from
such holocaust when the defensive system fails.

Discussion

Question: I would like to get your reaction to the Cornell University-University of Illinois no-solicitation pledge petition in which scientists pledge neither to solicit nor to accept money for SDI research. Over 1500 science and engineering faculty across the United States have signed the petition. This certainly does not indicate monolithic political acceptance of the program among the scientific community.

General Graham: I think the young man used the right term when he said "political acceptance." I said early on that this is not a technical problem. All of the problems that Professor Tsipis was laying are all being worked on by people who all believe they can be solved and are not just cynical people at the trough. They are working on solving them and I've talked to a lot of these people. What this young man's statement points out here is that what we're talking about here is politics. If you want to stay with mutual assured destruction and you want to bet on the di-plomats instead of the engineers, then you ought to sign that petition. But if you want to play the long suit of superior American technology to see if we can't get out of this situation, then you ought not to.

Dr. Tsipis: My concern is much more narrowly based. At the beginning of the Reagan administration, the fraction of the federally-provided R & D funds in this country that went for defense was about 48 percent. It is now nearing 70 per-cent. If SDI funds escalate as programmed, the fraction of federally-provided R & D funds that will go into defense projects will go perhaps to 80 percent. I am very much con-cerned about such a very large fraction of our resources being handled by a very few people who may or may not have good taste, as we say, in research and who certainly will have parochial rather than a nationally rational view of what good research is. So I'm concerned about that.

The other thing I'm concerned about is Japan spends 4 percent of its R & D on weapons, Germany spends 8 or 9 percent, France spends 10 percent, and we spend all that enormous fraction. I'm worried about the impact that this kind of policy will have on our ability to compete in international markets in the years to come. Our trade deficit, which is enormous, is not caused exclusively by this policy but this policy exacerbates what I think is a pretty dangerous situation of our falling further and further behind in technologies that are applicable to the civilian sector.

I've heard repeatedly the notion or the opinion that SDI research will have spinoffs that will be technologically exciting and also useful in the civilian sector. I have two comments on that. One is that if you want to spend money promoting research in the civilian sector you do that directly. You don't use the very inefficient approach of giving money to the military, hoping that some is going to fall off and help the civilian technology and our industrial and trade position in the world. Second, I have looked very closely at the technologies that SDI is supporting and promoting. I can think of only one that could potentially have enormously important civilian applications and that's the free-electron laser. I would be delighted to see all SDI money go to the free-electron laser because there is a device that, if perfected and understood better, could provide unbelieveable opportunities to the chemical industry, to all sorts of other things. Other applications of SDI are not in my mind applicable in the civilian sector.

Look for example at computers. SDI must have computers that are invulnerable to the electromagnetic pulse. We all know that electronic computers with their chips and their very low voltages can really be rattled by the electromagnetic pulse. We know that very well and we don't know even how to approach the problem of trying to correct that. Therefore computers for SDI will have to be optical computers, photonic computers. Now all of you know I am sure, you learned in fourth grade that optical elements are not as nonlinear as the electronic elements. Therefore switching times are much longer, more power is required. Thus optical computers will be much slower and much bigger and bulkier than the computers we have. Why on earth would anybody use them in civilian life? No one will. Thus even this

daunted approach that computer advances will occur because
of SDI is not true.

Question: Earlier General Abrahamson claimed that the SDI
program would encompass submarine- and bomber-launched
cruise missiles but Dr. Tsipis said otherwise. Why?

Dr. Tsipis: The SDI program as defined and as pursued now
is dealing exclusively with ballistic missiles. General
Abrahamson said that repeatedly and he, in my mind errone-
ously, pointed out that the ballistic missiles are the most
dangerous things that we face. I believe that cruise missiles and ballistic missiles from submarines, which have
very short flight times of six to eight minutes, and bombers can be as effective in attacking soft military targets
as ballistic missiles that come from the Soviet Union.

If you want to avoid a first-strike risk, you remove
your missiles from silos. You follow Senator Nunn's proposal of building single warhead missiles because it does
not pay to attack a single warhead missile. If both countries had single warhead missiles then it would be absolutely meaningless for the Soviets to attack our missiles
because they have to spend two of theirs to attack one of
ours. So you can remove the threat of a first strike from
the Soviet Union, which now exists, in ways other than
building an antiballistic missile shield. But SDI will do
nothing else but build an antiballistic missile shield.

In testimony in the Senate, Richard DeLauer, the undersecretary of defense for research and engineering, has
said that 90 percent of cruise missiles will penetrate.
Therefore clearly we do not have any protection, not only
of our cities and our industry, but also of our soft military targets. What are you going to do with an airfield?
You're not going to take it away. You have to leave it
there. You can take the planes off, but then where are they
going to land? So military targets are vulnerable to cruise
missiles and bombers the exact same way they are vulnerable
to ballistic missiles. The whole thing, it seems to me, is
not quite logical because even if you were to be effective
in stopping say 50 percent of the ballistic missiles, we
have very vulnerable cities, industries, and soft military
targets to other weapons.

What about silos? There are ways in which you can take
care of that other than building a ballistic missile defense. But if we decide to build a ballistic missile defense, then the kinds of technologies that we would be pursuing would not be the technologies that SDI is pursuing.

We would be pursuing quick-reaction, very fast ground-launched missiles. That's not something that the SDI is pursuing. General Abrahamson, who is an incredibly bright man and is highly respected by everyone because of that, sometimes talks from both sides of his mouth.

General Graham: The question is, does SDI lead also to defenses against other things? Of course it does because SDI is a change of strategy away from total reliance on offensive nuclear weapons to an emphasis on defending with non-nuclear systems. Once that strategy change is made the first thing you look at is what is the severe nuclear threat to the United States and our allies and that is long-range ballistic missiles. We are not really faced with a severe threat from cruise missiles and bombers because those are retaliatory weapons and the Soviets have not concentrated on them. They've concentrated on first-strike weapons which are the long-range ballistic missiles.

Now should the Soviets change their structure from an 85 percent emphasis on weapons that get here in thirty-five minutes to an emphasis instead on retaliatory weapons that get here in eight to sixteen hours (or weeks if you put them across the ocean in ships), then we would have to concentrate on that threat which is an easier technical problem than taking on the ballistic missile. So when General Abrahamson told you that, he was not talking out of both sides of his mouth, he was being the honest man he always is. He was saying that SDI does involve consideration of defenses against other systems when those other systems become a threat.

The real threat today of either deliberate or accidental nuclear war lies in the long-range ballistic missile against which we have zero defenses. We actually do have some defenses against bombers and cruise missiles. They are inadequate but there's not a big threat there and there is not going to be a first strike against this country with that kind of system or with nuclear weapons stuffed in a bale of marijuana or carried in by a wetback across the border somewhere.

Question: My question concerns nuclear winter. Assume that we have an effective multilayer defense system that will destroy most of the incoming missiles before they are detonated. However, a small percent of the total exchange will still penetrate and explode. With those assumptions, is nuclear winter still a problem for the people that survive?

General Graham: I believe in nuclear winter as much as some of Carl Sagan's colleagues who would disagree with me on everything else. It's atrocious science but it's good psychology from their political point of view. If you in fact believe in nuclear winter then you should be all aboard SDI, the reason being that in SDI our deterrent to nuclear war depends upon our creating nuclear winter. Now if you want to have a strategy that continues to rely on a system that will guarantee nuclear winter, then you ought to be aboard SDI. Either way you look at it you ought to be supporting SDI.

Dr. Tsipis: If the defensive shield as you describe it were to work, then you wouldn't have a problem with nuclear winter. General Graham is exactly right. The problem is that what probably will happen is that if we ever decide to erect such a shield, it is going to be imperfect and the simplest way for the Soviets to overcome it is to proliferate their offensive weapons. If we come to blows, what they will probably do is launch many, many more thousand weapons than they would have done without our defensive shield. Depending on how well our defensive shield would work, it may make things better or worse. If it works, it's going to cut down some of the Soviet weapons but if it doesn't, then you are going to have many more nuclear explosions coming from Soviet weapons over this country than otherwise. So if you are convinced that a defensive shield would work, then you don't have to worry about nuclear winter. But if you have any doubts, you better be concerned.

General Graham: But Kosta, I must interject here that what you are saying is that if the Soviets are going to react to defensive systems the way you think, they obviously don't believe in nuclear winter.

Question: My name is Richard Rusk, that last name is spelled R-U-S-K. General, you made a comparison between what you called the dismal record of the diplomats with the brilliant record of engineers and scientists and people like yourself. I don't begrudge you your positive self-image because it's important for people who advocate the SDI to have a positive self-image. There's another Rusk in the building who'll be speaking for himself later about the role of diplomacy in all of this. The record may have been dismal in places but I want to point out that forty years after Hiroshima and Nagasaki, we're still here. My question for you is, with all due respect for the patriotism and the good intentions of you and other people in the scientific community who believe in the SDI, what about the impact of this trillion dollars worth of research, development, and deployment on the degree of support that is being enlisted across the country?

Graham: Let me first mention something that Dean Rusk once said. He said that diplomacy only operates well in the shadow of military power. He was right about that. I wasn't trying to denigrate anybody who's been in the diplomatic business. I'm just telling you the diplomatic work for a free and open society where everybody and his dog is putting in their two bits worth as to exactly how that deal with the Soviet Union ought to go, our very system denies us the kind of effective diplomatic work that can be carried on by a von Ribbentrop and a Gromyko.

Regarding suggestions that all this support is being purchased by the government's research program -- I'll tell you that the support was out there before the president ever sounded off. We have polled the American public and asked them if they approved or disapproved of space-borne defenses against Soviet long-range ballistic missiles and the answers always come in three- or four-to-one yes despite whether the person calls himself Republican, Democrat, Independent, Liberal, Conservative, Moderate. It comes in at very strong support levels. That the same kind of strong support is evident in the scientific and technical community is not strange. As a matter of fact it does not surprise me that it's even greater among the technical people than among others because they understand these things. And they understand what can be done and they understand, of course, that their interest in technology in general is important. This is the very important part of this issue.

The Soviet objections to SDI are not just a matter of losing a military advantage. What they are worried about is this great engineering and scientific community of the free world with all the enormous advantages it has over the Soviet system. This will move the whole free world onto a new technological plateau in which the Soviet system is simply noncompetitive. Yes, there are people who are interested in this because they are interested in technology in general. But no, their support has not been bought by the government of the United States.

Question: Some SDI concepts involve the use of the so-called x-ray laser energized by nuclear explosions.

Please comment on the degree to which SDI needs and possibly other nuclear applications within SDI may be inhibiting the attempt to reach a comprehensive nuclear test ban agreement.

General Graham: I don't know that it is having any effect on the comprehensive nuclear test ban treaty. That's mostly an argument about verification. The president has called for a non-nuclear system. Of course an argument could be made that what they're talking about in the x-ray laser arena is not a nuclear weapon and you can't hurt anybody with it but it does cause a political problem. This is why you get a lot of stress on it in the anti-SDI side of the house. They love to stress that weapon. As a matter of fact, I don't know whether Dr. Tsipis was part of the action, but a number of other noted scientists said they would be all for SDI if the administration would go for the nuclear option. I think they were playing pure politics because they know if they could insert a nuclear device that was going to be up in space they would destroy public support for the system.

My opposition to the x-ray system is basically the simple military paradox it creates. If you put it up there in a satellite and the only way it can defend itself is to explode itself, you've created a military paradox. It's like putting a sentry out and the only way he protects his post is to pull a pin on a hand grenade that blows himself up and catches the intruder. That's kind of a bad way to do business in my book. This also has caused a man whom I respect and admire a great deal, Dr. Edward Teller, to say some things that were quoted by Dr. Tsipis. Back in April 1983, Dr. Teller said he didn't want it in space to avoid that paradox and wanted it deployed on the ground and popped up into space.

I approve of continued research on the x-ray laser but it is outside of the demand of the president of the United States which is for a non-nuclear system. I believe when he says non-nuclear, he means non-nuclear powered and not involving nuclear devices of any sort. For my own part, if I thought that it made a lot of military sense, I would be all for using the x-ray laser. But I do have some serious doubts about its applicability in the defense of the United States. It may turn out to be one of the best ways, however, to do the same thing for Europe in the European Defense Initiative that's just been launched by a group of distinguished European officials who are figuring out how to go with the inevitable move of the United States into strategic defenses and do it with particular emphasis on the defensive requirements of Europe. They may indeed use the x-ray laser Excalibur system.

Dr. Tsipis: The x-ray laser is a 100 kiloton nuclear explosive that pumps a very thin fiber of zinc and induces it to produce a burst of soft x-rays. Therefore it is very much a nuclear device. It is not very promising on purely physical grounds and therefore it is not a favored project of the Strategic Defense Initiative Organization. The laboratories, however, and Mr. Teller are strenuously arguing against the test ban precisely because they want to develop the x-ray laser and other so-called "third generation" nuclear weapons. So one of the arguments against the complete test ban is the presence of this device and the hope that at some point it may become a useful weapon.

There is every reason to believe that it will never become a weapon against a ballistic missile because you can protect a ballistic missile and because it is very difficult to get the kinds of performance that you need. On the other hand, the arguments that have swayed past presidents against signing a complete test ban treaty do come from the laboratories and are based on the claim that new devices must be developed and that requires testing.

PART THREE

SDI and Arms Control

5

New Wine in Old Bottles: The Reagan Administration's "New Interpretation" of the ABM Treaty

Gerard C. Smith

I am reminded of a little story Senator Sam Nunn told. There was a man who spent his whole life studying the Johnstown Flood. When he succeeded in getting to heaven, St. Peter said it was usual for new entrants to speak and asked what subject the man would speak about. The man said he would like to talk about the Johnstown flood since he was the greatest expert in the world on that. St. Peter said that would be fine, but he should know that Noah would be in the audience.

We have heard a good deal about diplomats versus engineers. I would like to hazard the suggestion that one of our difficulties especially in regard to SDI, is that it is based on calculations basically made by scientists and engineers on a diplomatic subject. The whole premise of SDI, even by its advocates, is that the Soviets will cooperate with us to make our defensive problem more manageable. This is seen as an inducement to the Soviets going in for arms control. That is a basic miscalculation and it was basically made by people who have had no experience in the arms control business. Rather they are following a scientific sort of logic that said to them that, if we really demonstrate that we can make Soviet missiles obsolete and impotent, the Soviets will come around and negotiate with us. So far, I am sorry to say, that has not proved to be the case at all. In fact the opposite has proved to be the case. The lesson for me is that the engineers should stick to their lasts and the diplomats should stick to theirs. There is plenty of room for both of them to work on this field of national security.

We hear a great deal about what America could do about improving its defenses but we do not hear much about the other side. My personal preference is that since the Soviets now are virtually defenseless in the face of our ballistic missiles, I would like to see them kept that way. I think the security of the United States is better if the Soviets are defenseless. But the administration's plan is not that way. They welcome the addition of defenses to the Soviet forces. In fact we have heard what seems to me the absurd notion that we are going to sell our technology to the Soviets to help them make our missiles impotent and obsolete. That brings back memories to me of the days when we were selling scrap iron to the Japanese and it came to us in a form we did not like at all.

My general thesis is that defense, or as I like to put it developing weapons to counter ballistic missiles, has been bad for past arms control and is even worse for the prospect of future arms control. I think that if you look at the past record you see the erosion of the ABM Treaty. Now this is not all our fault by any means. The Soviets have taken part in this exercise. But the treaty has been wounded. I know that there are new interpretations of the ABM Treaty which strike me as evidence of what the SDI is doing to the structure of arms control. It clearly foreshadows a more permissive attitude towards development and testing of systems that we thought we had prevented in the ABM Treaty. It reflects the tensions that are existing between what the engineers want to do and what the lawyers or former lawyers used to think they were not supposed to do.

I do not want to go into that matter. The administration and I have had our day in court before congressional committees. I have the feeling that the die is cast, the administration has made its opinion, there is no court of appeal. I think the opinion is dead wrong but the only way to get any surcease from this is if the administration or some future administration starts to spend money based on this new legal theory. Then I suspect there will be a justiciable issue. I will be very interested in those days to see how the courts will treat this question of the unilateral amendment of a treaty.

SDI has had the effect of stretching the meaning of the ABM Treaty even under the old version. I know that my friends in the administration do not like me to call it the traditional version, so let us call it the version that obtained from 1972 to 1985. The SDI program calls for testing starting in 1988 which clearly seems to me to trench upon the treaty. They call for work outside the laboratory, work that I do not think under any old-fashioned concept of research can be considered true research. It is clearly

development work and testing work and testing in outer
space and testing from aircraft. It represents another case
where SDI is stretching the arms control process.

We have also been told that we can probably start developing ballistic missile defenses under the guise of developing satellite killer systems or anti-tactical ballistic missile systems which are not covered by the treaty.
Those are two substantial loopholes certainly in the case
of anti-tactical ballistic missiles, loopholes left at our
specific request. We had a system, now called the Patriot
surface-to-air missile system, to defend against aircraft
that we wanted to keep in the open. It had a potential a-
gainst tactical ballistic missiles but nevertheless we did
not want to constrain it. Now we are faced with the fact
that there is a large overlap in the technology between
those weapons and antiballistic missile systems. I gather
that the administration plans to drive as much technology
through that loophole as they can.

In general as a lawyer I would call the whole strategic defense program an anticipatory breach of contract. We
have a treaty that is the supreme law of the land and it
says "Thou shalt not deploy a nationwide defense." This is
unconditional language but that is what we are trying to
do. I do not see how you can avoid saying that that is not
an anticipatory breach of the ABM Treaty.

The Soviets clearly are doing a great deal of work in
this field. I contrast the president's statement that they
are ten years ahead of us with General Abrahamson's statement that in the five key ares of this technology that we
are far, far ahead. This is also one of the troubles that
SDI is giving us. It is leading to exaggerated claims in
order to get public support and congressional support for
funding the SDI. There is an element of pretense that this
is just research, that the Soviets are way ahead, and what
we are really doing is just trying to catch up. As Senator
Nunn indicated in a more diplomatic fashion than I, there
is an element of deceit in all this. When the American people wake up and realize this is not a population defense,
the reaction and backlash can be very strong.

Looking for a minute at the possibilities in Geneva, I
feel that there is no prospect of getting new arms control
agreements until we can clean up the situation about existing agreements. I do not see how we can go along charging
the Soviets with cheating and having them countercharge
with our cheating and yet say we want to make new agreements. We have to do something about the past agreements.
That is why I welcome the Soviet statement that they would

offer to stop construction of their big Siberian radar. The deal they offered is not realistic, i.e., that we would trade two of our big early warning radars for their Krasno-yarsk radar. But the fact that they would even raise the subject is a good signal. We could work out an arrangement that handled these large phased array radar questions. We recognized in negotiating that treaty in 1972 that this was one of the slipperiest things that we were trying to get hold of. We realized that we had not made a perfect solu-tion of it. There are ways now where we could get something that would reassure both sides on the big radar question.

By the same token the whole question of the future of the ABM Treaty is tied up with SALT II, the controls on offensive weapons that we never ratified. One of the big questions there is our charge that the Soviets have deve-loped two new ICBMs whereas they are only permitted to have one under the treaty. By the same token, we have in mind doing the same thing with the MX and the Midgetman. It seems to me not beyond the ingenuity of man to reconcile those two positions. If we really want to have two ICBMs then we ought to be able to work out some sort of an ar-rangement that would clear the air.

The other significant claim is that the Soviets are encrypting telemetry which is impeding our ability to veri-fy what they are doing. I think this is a serious charge. But you should remember that this is in connection with a treaty that the United States has refused to ratify. In effect we are saying that the Soviets are violating an un-ratified treaty by not making our verfication tasks some-what easier. I think that it would not take very much, given political will, for the Soviets without a new agree-ment to cut back on the amount of encryption they are do-ing. They have us in a box because they say "You say we are impeding your ability to verify. What is it you need?" We cannot answer that question because that would give away the limitations on our intelligence, so we just step away from that question. But there are solutions to that sort of a problem.

As far as the future is concerned I feel we have a great dilemma because we are trying at the Geneva negoti-ations to control offensive weapons and at the same time decontrol, or at least keep open an option to decontrol, defensive weapons. That is a stance that seems illogical to me and we cannot maintain it for very long. We say that SDI brought the Soviets back to the table. Technically that cannot be right because when the SDI was announced in March 1983, the Soviets were still at the table and stayed there

for six months after that. I grant that the SDI is having a
constructive effect on the mentality of the Soviets to get
on with arms control. But what do we now say, having
brought them back to the table to negotiate? We are saying
about SDI for them to go away for about ten or twenty years
and when we have developed these defenses, then come back
and we will negotiate about how to integrate them into our
offensive weaponry. That is not a positon we can handle for
very long.

We are talking about banning mobile missiles in our
latest offer. This is about the third time we have changed
our mind about whether mobile missiles are good or bad for
us. I have a feeling this latest decision is a rather tactical move, not seriously thought through from the national
security point of view. I think it reflects a calculation
that Congress might not support money for a mobile missile
so it might be better to get the Soviets to ban them. The
Soviets have two mobile systems that they are about to deploy. It would be nice if we got to choke them off by
agreement.

By the same token, banning mobile missiles would be a
plus for SDI. Mobile missiles are an alternative to SDI
when it comes to protecting our ICBMs in silos. If we could
put those ICBMs in a mobile mode, you would not have to
have this early stage of strategic defense which is hard-
point defense or defense of silos. Thus the mobile move is
directly related to the question of SDI.

The president has said that SDI would be the greatest
inducement to arms reduction. But the record does not suggest that at all. The Soviets right from the start said
absolutely not. And now they are facing us with a dilemma:
Do you want sharp reductions in offensive weapons or do you
want to persist in trying to mount a big strategic defense?
That must be an agonizing decision for the president to
make because it is a question of a bird in the hand or two
in the bush, with the two in the bush being maybe twenty
years in the future. I think he really wants to have an
arms control agreement. Whereas I am pessimistic about the
summit, in general I have some small hope that a signal
will be given that if the Soviet offer is sweet enough,
although it is not now but it could become that, then we
would be willing to reach some agreement limiting in some
respect the development and testing work, but not research,
being done on SDI.

I have long been a very strong proponent of a major
research program in strategic defenses for two reasons --
as an insurance policy against a Soviet breakout or

creepout from the ABM Treaty and the other as an aid to our intelligence. We cannot really understand our intelligence about the Soviet programs unless we have done these experiments ourselves. This is a very important reason for a continuing program.

Let me close with a few general observations. I think the administration's push for weapons to counter ballistic missiles is confusing if not deceiving the American people. The prospect of eliminating nuclear weapons makes SDI appear as something of a substitute for arms control. Its prospect of protecting our population from nuclear attack makes the present situation seem somewhat more tolerable, as just an interim stage before scientists and engineers put an end to the postwar period of nuclear danger. This easing of anxieties makes the absence of more arms control seem acceptable. I do not believe that the professional SDI people are true believers in this exaggerated version of the future but that is how SDI is perceived by the public from hearing and reading the administration's rhetoric. In the claim that the Soviets are ten years ahead of us in strategic defense, we are resorting to an extravagance to get funding that can only backfire when the facts become known.

We have a clear choice to try to reduce by mutual agreement the strategic forces of both sides or to develop weapons to counter just one type of nuclear threat, ballistic missiles. I doubt that we can control offensive forces while developing this option which would require decontrol of defensive forces. And I am concerned that we will end up with neither arms control nor the president's vision nor anything like it but with an indefinite competition in both offensive and defensive forces.

6

The ABM Treaty
and the SDI Program

Abraham D. Sofaer

When one is interpreting a treaty for the purpose of determining whether the United States of America is bound by that treaty with respect to one type of activity or another, it is very important, even indispensable, to look carefully at the language of the treaty, to give it a fair and reasonable construction, to look at the negotiating record, and to be responsible about this whole process. What is the bottom line on this process? The bottom line is the question: Are you going to tell your client, the President of the United States, that he is bound not to test or develop space-based technology when a fair reading of the ABM Treaty and the negotiating record reflects that the Soviet Union cannot be said to be bound by those same limitations? You have to apply, in this area of treaty interpretation, the basic principle of mutual obligations. This principle applies to international agreements just as it applies to local agreements between you and your landlord, between you and your university. If one side is not bound by certain interpretations of a treaty, it is incumbent upon a lawyer to tell his client he is not bound either.

I want to concentrate on this point because it will not help you nor would it be meaningful educationally to summarize the very interesting issues of SDI and all the wonderful things that could happen or could be projected. It would be more meaningful to go through the ABM Treaty to show how untenable, and certainly untenable relative to a broader view, is this restrictive view we have been told about by Ambassador Gerard Smith, that some have very loosely characterized as the "authoritative" interpretation of the United States from 1972 to the present.

The ABM Treaty is an important element in our strategic arms control structure. When the president first announced the SDI program, he made it clear that it would be conducted in accordance with our obligations under that treaty. This commitment has been maintained. The United States has scrupulously complied notwithstanding such clear Soviet violations as the Krasnoyarsk radar station. Soviet violations of the treaty, the SDI program, and the ongoing negotiations at Geneva where this issue has been discussed recently caused various agencies of the executive branch to look harder at the meaning of the ABM Treaty than they had before. We were asked what the impact of the treaty was upon future or exotic systems. By that I mean defensive systems that serve the same functions as ABM systems and components but that use devices based on physical principles other than those used in 1972 when the treaty was negotiated. These systems would be capable of substituting for ABM interceptor missiles, launchers, and radars.

This examination led to the conclusion that a reading of the ABM Treaty that would allow the development and testing of such systems based on physical principles other than those used in 1972 is wholly justified. At the same time I want to emphasize a critical point made by Secretary of State George Shultz in his speech to the North Atlantic Assembly when he said, "Our SDI research program has been structured, as the president has reaffirmed, and will continue to be conducted in accordance with a restrictive interpretation of the treaty's obligations." So the issue we are talking about is not an issue that relates to whether or not, whichever way you come out on this question, we are violating the ABM Treaty. That is not the question and it is wholly moot. We are doing nothing now that would violate the treaty even if you do accept the restrictive version. We have concluded, however, that the restrictive version is not the correct reading of the ABM Treaty.

We were well aware when we began this work that several officials associated with the SALT I negotiations and others still in the government had advanced the view that the ABM Treaty is unambiguous in its treatment of such future systems. They argued that Article V of the treaty forbids the development, testing, or deployment of any future ABM systems and components other than those that are fixed, land-based. They read Agreed Statement D as relevant only to fixed, land-based systems and components, arguing that it permits creation of such systems and components when they are based on other physical principles but conditions their deployment on agreement between the parties on specific limitations. My study of the treaty led me to conclude that its language is ambiguous and can in fact more reasonably be read to support a broader interpretation.

The restrictive view rests on the premise that Article V(1) is clear on its face. It says there will be no development, testing, or deployment of "ABM systems or components" other than those that are fixed, land-based. But this language does not settle the issue of the article's applicability to future systems or components. That issue depends on the meaning of the term "ABM systems or components." Is that phrase limited to systems and components based on then-current technology or does it also include those based on other physical principles? To answer this question you have to turn to Article II(1). Proponents of the restrictive view contend that the definition of ABM system in that article is functional, i.e., anything ever conceived that could serve the function of countering strategic missiles in flight falls within the definition. They argue that the three components identified in Article II(1) -- missiles, launchers, and ABM radars -- are merely listed as elements that an ABM system currently consists of and that all future components of a system that satisfies the functional definition are also covered by Article II(1). It is this meaning of Article II(1) that gives proponents of the restrictive view the logical basis for claiming that Article V is a total ban on testing and development of future systems and components.

This reading of the treaty is plausible. Judges I know in cases have come up with all sorts of readings as plausible. It is very difficult to say that a reading is implausible on its face. But it is not the only reasonable reading. On the contrary, it has serious shortcomings. The premise that Article II(1) defines ABM system in a functional manner meant to include all future systems and components is difficult to sustain. The provision can more reasonably be read to mean that the systems contemplated by the treaty are those that serve the functions described and that currently consist of the listed components. In fact the treaty's other provisions insofar as they use the phrase "ABM system or component" all refer to then-existing systems and components.

Systems and components based on future technology are not discussed anywhere in the treaty other than in Agreed Statement D. In that provision the parties felt a need to qualify the term "systems and components created in the future" with the phrase "based on other physical principles." If "ABM systems and components" actually meant all systems or devices that could serve ABM functions, whether based on present or future technology, the parties would not have needed to qualify these terms in Agreed Statement D. It is only because they do not mean and were not intended to cover future unknown technologies that the parties saw a need to use this additional qualifying term.

Furthermore, the very existence of Agreed Statement D poses a fundamental problem for those who advocate this restrictive view. Nothing in that statement suggests that it applies only to future systems that are fixed, land-based. On the contrary, it addresses all ABM systems and components that are based on other physical principles. The restrictive interpretation would render Agreed Statement D superfluous.

Stop to read the treaty and consider the meanings that you have to attribute to these articles in order to reach the restrictive view. You have Article II(1) extending to all ABM systems and components based on present as well as future technology. But then you have Article III implicitly banning everything but the fixed, land-based systems that it permits. If that were the case there was absolutely no purpose then to writing Agreed Statement D. Indeed that interpretation undercuts the very meaning and purpose of Article V itself. That is because if Article III by using the words "ABM system and components" was meant to refer to all ABM systems and components ever conceived present or future, there would have been no need for these additional prohibitions.

When you interpret a treaty, if you have a clause that is rendered superfluous by a proposed interpretation, it is not a favored interpretation. I would suggest that the interpretation that the administration has adopted harmonizes all the provisions of the treaty and creates a logical and entirely reasonable structure for the regulation of present and future systems of all sorts.

I want to address the second point. We hear repeatedly said "Thirteen years of consistent view suddenly has been changed." There is no such thing. It is true that in the last two or three years, since the SDI program was advanced, the Department of Defense and other agencies and some government officials have advanced the restrictive view of the treaty. That is clear and no one can contest that. But it is untrue to say that this restrictive view has been uniformly advanced even recently, and indeed it is true to say that almost every single statement made about this treaty during the period of its ratification, from 1972 all the way up to 1979, are either consistent with the broader view of the treaty that I am advancing or indeed support the broader view. And I include in that all the statements made by Ambassador Gerard Smith himself. Whenever he said anything about the treaty's applicability to future systems, he referred to Agreed Statement D and only to Agreed Statement D. Virtually no one referred to Article V as an absolute ban on future devices. When the subject of future devices came up, people turned to and talked about Agreed Statement D and only Agreed Statement D.

It is possible and it would be ironic to say, quite to the contrary of what Ambassador Smith has contended, that the SDI program has generated this change of interpretation. In fact, if you look at this as objective students of the treaty and of the way the political system in the United States works, the SDI program may have generated the narrower view rather than the broader view. The position may have been generated by people who oppose the SDI program and do not ever want to see it extended beyond a research program, and by people who support the SDI program and want to paint it as being limited by some external principle that governs its future growth. I cannot tell that that is how it happened but I can suggest these possibilities as possible hypotheses that are far more tenable than Ambassador Smith's suggestion that the administration has been motivated in this interpretation of the ABM Treaty by a desire to leave room for future development of the SDI program.

Finally I would add that the Soviets themselves never publicly asserted the restrictive view until the United States announced the broader view as its authoritative view of the ABM Treaty. The Soviets claimed that the SDI program would violate the treaty because it would lead to the deployment of new ABM-type systems. The implicit learning in this is that they, too, have regarded the ABM Treaty as limiting the deployment of future systems but not their testing and development. Of course they have jumped on the bandwagon now and claim we are violating the treaty also by testing and developing. But the record reflects that this is a recent development.

I think this a worthwhile debate. It is important to go into the details of some of the technicalities and I urge everyone to do so before you reach your conclusions. But I want to re-emphasize that the president is conducting the SDI program in accordance with Ambassador Smith's wishes. It is a research program and the public and the

64

Congress will have plenty of opportunity to decide to move forward into testing and development if and when that time ever comes.

7

Reconciling SDI with American Treaty Commitments

Christopher C. Joyner

The question of SDI all too easily demonstrates a fundamental reality of our modern times, namely the profound difficulty which the process of international law has in keeping up with, much less regulating, the phenomenal leaps in contemporary technological advancement. Even so there is a body of available international law that clearly is relevant and applicable to arms control and particularly the Strategic Defense Initiative.

The general focus of my remarks therefore will be on international law and to outline generally the relevant tenets of international law which are affected by the SDI program. In doing so I would also like to conclude by making some remarks about the recent controversy concerning the revised interpretation by the Reagan administration of the ABM Treaty as well as the implications that reinterpretation might pose for arms control.

With respect to the Strategic Defense Initiative in international law, there are two principle treaties that stand out as being particularly relevant. The first is the Outer Space Treaty of 1967. The United States and the Soviet Union are both parties to that fundamental commitment. The Outer Space Treaty of 1967 is widely regarded as being the foundation of space law and therefore is the paramount document concerning the peaceful use of outer space. It stems from two United Nations General Assembly resolutions in 1961 and 1963. Articles I and II of the Outer Space Treaty state that space activities, of which SDI would likely be one, should be conducted in accordance with international law and explicitly refers to the United Nations Charter in that regard. With regard to the Strategic Defense Initiative, Article IV of the Outer Space Treaty has special relevance. The first paragraph merits quotation:

"States Parties to the Treaty undertake not to place in orbit around the Earth any objects carrying nuclear weapons or any other kinds of weapons of mass destruction, install such weapons on celestial bodies, or station such weapons in outer space in any other manner." In my view directed-energy weapons as scientifically envisaged at the present time would not constitute nuclear weapons as conceived by this provision of the Outer Space Treaty. SDI weapons have a limited specific target; thus one can properly argue that they do not accurately represent weapons of mass destruction as well. In my view therefore directed-energy weapons such as lasers or charged or neutral particle beams may be deemed outside the scope of the prohibitions in the Outer Space Treaty. One can agree also that the treaty prohibits only stationing such weapons in space, not their development or deployment on earth nor even the deployment of ground-based nuclear systems designed to be used against space objects. There are serious implications here also for SDI and these should not be overlooked.

The treaty goes on to note a number of provisions about the moon and celestial bodies. While those are not really relevant for SDI purposes it should be mentioned that also in Article IV reference is made in paragraph two to "peaceful purposes," an allusion which also appears in the Preamble of the treaty. In this regard, the interpretation of "peaceful purposes" within any treaty context stands out for me as a critical one. The expression "peaceful purposes" interestingly enough has been described as a legal term of art; that is, the United States government and the Soviet Union's government do not interpret that phrase to mean the same thing. For the United States, we have defined "peaceful" as meaning "nonaggressive," and thus applicable to the definition of outer space and the activities there. For the Soviet Union, "peaceful" is equated with being non-military, and thus the Soviet Union applies this interpretation to outer space. There is important consideration here as well in whether SDI will be viewed as a peaceful use of outer space. The Soviets would argue that it is not a peaceful use but a military use, while the United States would describe it as a defensive use of outer space and therefore not aggressive in its intention.

The second principle treaty relating to the SDI is the ABM Treaty of 1972. Article II of the treaty defines an ABM system as currently consisting of ABM interceptor missiles, ABM launchers, and ABM radars. In my view, the text does not preclude treaty jurisdiction over future ABM systems

using devices other than those mentioned. The key question
turns on whether the drafters of this section intended to
include such systems. This indeed is the recent debate. In
this regard, Agreed Statement D becomes the focal point of
contention. It mandates consultations between the Soviet
Union and the United States which should be undertaken in
the event new ABM devices such as SDI are contemplated. I
would hope that such consultations might be forthcoming
within that context.

Let me remind you also that Article V(1) of the ABM
Treaty provides the following, which I view as the critical
provision of the treaty: "Each Party undertakes not to develop, test, or deploy ABM systems or components which are
sea-based, air-based, space-based, or mobile land-based."
While it is true the ABM Treaty contains some ambiguous
language, I find this article to be perfectly clear. The
treaty thus distinguishes between ABM systems according to
their basing modes. It also indicates clearly that no development, testing, or deployment should be undertaken except for fixed, land-based systems which are defined in the
treaty. For me this provision entails a cardinal restriction in international law against the SDI proposal as presently conceived should it pass the research phase.

Importantly, however, while the treaty precludes development of ABM devices, research is not specifically addressed. As we all know, where research ends and development begins is frequently an unclear area. But both the
United States and the Soviet Union are known now to be en-
gaged in basic research regarding directed-energy weapons
and antisatellite weaponry. Largely for that reason, I too
would join in the advocation that we continue research
along these lines although when it comes to testing, development, and deployment, a great amount of caution should be
exercised before those decisions are undertaken.

Important too for all of us to realize is that the ABM
Treaty contains both amendment provisions as well as withdrawal provisions. The United States therefore has the option to withdraw from the ABM Treaty or in fact work to
negotiate with the Soviets to amend it to allow for SDI.
Obviously that latter proposal seems incredulous at the
present time.

In discussing the international legal implications of
SDI aside from the Outer Space Treaty and the ABM Treaty,
there are a number of other important international legal
instruments which have been promulgated and are now in
force which are binding upon the United States and the Soviet Union that would be affected by SDI. The Partial Test

Ban Treaty which has been signed by both the superpowers in 1963 specifically prohibits in Article I any nuclear tests or explosions in outer space. That provision might limit the deployment of such weapons in an SDI program. The Accident Measures Agreement of 1971 and the Agreement on the Prevention of Nuclear War of 1973 together obligate the United States and the Soviet Union to refrain from interfering with each other's early warning systems. These agreements are intended to protect satellites which are components of such early warning systems from antisatellite aggression. What I mean to suggest here is that if SDI was used as an antisatellite device, it might might become a device abrogating those agreements. The 1973 International Telecommunications Convention and Protocol also contain several general regulations which limit radio frequency interference with satellites. This too might come into play should SDI be used as a space-based weapon against satellites. The 1977 Environmental Modification Convention prohibits certain environmental modification techniques affecting outer space. Were SDI to be employed to be used to destroy missiles, obviously a case could be made that this was contributing to the pollution of outer space although I do not think any of us would worry about that. However, the relevance of the provisions are still there because this could affect the world's ecology and indeed could have impacts upon nuclear winter.

Finally let me mention the 1979 Moon Treaty only in passing. It does have peaceful uses only of outer space and the moon contained within its provisions. However the United States and the Soviet Union are neither signatories nor parties to this particular treaty and therefore would not be bound by its commitments in any event.

In summary I want to mention some conclusions arising from my research on SDI's role in international law. If research conducted under SDI were to develop laser and particle beam weapons and if the testing were successful and resulted in development or deployment in outer space, two conclusions can be drawn. First, a supportable argument can be presented that the United States would not technically contravene any portion of the Outer Space Treaty since directed-energy weapons represent neither nuclear weapons nor weapons of mass destruction. In the same vein, the second conclusion is that the United States would be in clear violation of that portion of Article V of the ABM Treaty which limits ABM defense measures to stationary, land-based modes. Also, based upon the agreed interpretations of the ABM Treaty, it seems obvious that the negotiators intended to include future systems that might be developed in addition to those that might be defined in the treaty. Nevertheless it is neither clear nor certain that the ABM Treaty was intended to prohibit research in future systems. Thus one may conclude that no violation would occur while the SDI program remains in the research stage. But the fine line between research and development is vague and ambiguous, creating a slippery problem which must be dealt with later regarding the legal implications of SDI.

A second fundamental conclusion is that satellite space systems in the contemporary technological era contribute significantly to self-defense and well as deterrence and arms control. Antisatellite activity directed at satellites performing another state's national technical means of verification would violate agreements made at the time of SALT I and SALT II. However I should note that neither agreement today is legally binding upon either party.

The third major conclusion is that given the legal right of states to be able to provide adequate means of self-preservation and national defense, the recognized Soviet doctrine of remaining at least equal to the United States in the area of armaments, and the U.S. intelligence evidence which indicates significant Soviet progress along the lines of directed-energy weapons, it seems unlikely to me that new international agreements will be reached in the very near term which would prohibit either the United States or the Soviet Union from ultimately acquiring directed-energy weapons which might be based in space or used against space objects. I sincerely hope I am wrong on that count. But in order for such agreements to be forthcoming, there is going to have to be greater conciliation, a greater sense of understanding, and trust by both governments coupled with significant means of verification.

My final comments deal with the recent debate over the reinterpretation of the ABM Treaty. The Reagan administration on October 28, 1985, confirmed that it had adopted a new interpretation of the ABM Treaty. This interpretation, suggested by security adviser Robert McFarlane, holds that testing and development of exotic energy weapons are permissible under the 1972 agreement. The rationale for this revised interpretation rests in Agreed Statement D. The purpose of this statement originally allowed the two parties to maintain a conventional ABM system. In the event ABM systems based on other physical properties were created in the future, specific limitations on such systems and their components would be subject to discussion. Thus the crux of this issue hangs on whether Agreed Statement D supplies a sufficiently broad exemption from the treaty's restriction to permit a future type of ABM system "based on other physical principles" such as lasers and directed-energy weapons.

For me the administration's reinterpretation of the ABM Treaty's provisions does not alter my primary conclusions. I believe it is faulty and misguided to argue that the agreed statement appended to the treaty text can supersede the clear, unambiguous language of Article V, i.e., that each party undertakes not to develop, test, or deploy ABM systems or components which are sea-based, air-based, space-based, or mobile land-based. For me such reinterpretation also invites opening the Pandora's box of evils that the ABM Treaty is supposed to contain and would in fact legitimize the very Soviet ABM defensive activities which the United States and the Reagan administration have been so critical and fearful of. In my opinion, the lawfulness of the administration's new policy position seems shaky. The conclusion that I reach is reinforced by previous statements I have found in the public domain by the treaty negotiators. Additionally the public legal positions espoused by the Nixon, Ford, Carter, and Reagan administrations up until October 8, 1985, have maintained that testing and deployment of an ABM system using lasers and directed-energy weapons and other exotic space-based weapons are restricted by the ABM Treaty. Obviously the redefined position of the administration reflects policy posturing by the administration in order to prepare for the summit.

In my view, over the short term one can argue that such revised interpretations will work politically to our bargaining advantage. In the long term, however, I am concerned. In the long term such convenient interpretive revisions undercut our diplomatic credibility. They also serve to strain the negotiating confidence that must be present for any arms control agreement to be successfully obtained by the superpowers. My reservations about the reinterpretation were borne out when Secretary of State George Schultz announced on October 14, 1985, that President Reagan had chosen to take a narrower interpretation of the treaty, in effect returning to the policy position in accordance with the treaty's original obligations as it had been interpreted throughout the 1970s until 1985. That notwithstanding, the point bears noting that the administration maintains that it is now "respecting some of the most important restrictions on the ABM Treaty as a matter of presidential policy rather than a matter of law." For me,

in dealing with matters affecting arms control, I wish that
it might have been the other way around.

Discussion

Question: While I will graciously avoid the temptation to
question the sincerity of Judge Sofaer, I wish merely to
point out he is the chief legal counsel of the U.S. Department of State. As I understand it, any counsel is required,
if he takes the job, to represent the interest of his client. Given that the very purpose of the ABM Treaty was to
proscribe the sort of comprehensive ballistic missile defense envisioned by the SDI, is it any wonder that the administration is able to find counsel which will defend its
necessary and novel reinterpretation of the treaty? Since
the author of the treaty is present, I would ask his further comment on possible adverse implications of this reinterpretation.

Ambassador Smith: I think the purpose of treaties is to
lend some degree of predictability in international relations. If a treaty can be treated rather cavalierly after
thirteen years the predictability is dissipated. I think
that is very unfortunate. In the future people doing business with us are bound to say, "How long will the United
States live with a treaty until it decides it is more convenient to say it means something else?" For instance, suppose we took a position that the NATO treaty didn't mean
what we thought it meant for a long time. This would cause
a great deal of structural problems in the alliance. I
think the very fact that it was the protest of our close
allies, according to press reports, that led to this retraction of the new version is the best evidence of what
this sort of tampering with the treaty is bound to lead to.

Judge Sofaer: First let me say that I hope people will
read the treaty's provisions and deal with the facts.

If you look at the facts and you look at the treaty and you
look at the record of the public statements made, all of
which we have collected and put into memoranda and put before you, you will see that the statements that have been
made about this so-called reinterpretation are groundless.
The fact is that there has been no retraction for example
by Secretary Schultz or President Reagan of this interpretation of the treaty. Just those statements alone should
give you some clue of the fact that some people want to see
in statements what they believe, and they see it no matter
what the facts are.

PART FOUR

Political-Diplomatic Issues

8

SDI and the NATO Allies

Martin J. Hillenbrand

Anyone who listens to the wide variety of disparate views which have been expressed about the interpretation of the ABM Treaty, which could only puzzle the average listener as to where the truth lies, cannot be surprised when I say that the European audience is equally nonplussed and confused about the precise meaning and implications of the Strategic Defense Initiative. It is fair to say that our handling of the alliance in this context has been rather inept, starting with Secretary Weinberger's sixty-day ultimatum to the allies during which they were to meditate over the subject and then let him know whether they were interested in joining in the research part of the program.

It is fair to say that the Europeans, at least the governments, to a degree are torn between two disparate and somewhat paradoxical realities. First of all, many of them are tempted to cash in on what promises to be what a German official described to me as "one of the richest pork barrels in history." At the same time there is a fear of radical change possibly resulting from the SDI in the strategic posture of the United States. I think the motives as far as the first aspect is concerned are quite clear. They are not all that different from those which have been attributed to the American scientific community. That is, if the money is there, why not get a share of it? Some European governments, particularly the research and development aspects of those governments, have been tempted by this despite their feeling that Mr. Weinberger was being arbitrary and insulting by his deadline.

Based on my recent visit to a number of European capitals and talking to a number of officials there who are concerned with this problem, there are a number of questions that Europeans raise. First of all there is the

question of what the SDI means, given the conflicting definitions of the program that have come out of Washington,
some from the mouth of the president and some from the
mouths of other spokesmen for the administration. They sup-
plement that question by raising another question of whether the SDI actually in practice boils down to the defense
of a few missile silos rather than being a more comprehensive shield or "astrodome". There is a second question that
the Europeans ask -- What about the post-Reagan era? After
all, they know that President Reagan will be president only
until the beginning of 1989. They wonder whether there will
be any continuity in this program beyond that time once his
personal support and obvious engagement in this program
disappears. It appears that the program will generate
enough momentum so this fear is not very substantial.

A more significant European fear is their tendency to
link the SDI to what they would regard as a progressive
decoupling of the U.S. strategic deterrent from the defense
of Europe. Of course they are not intimately acquainted
with all of the cast of characters in Washington who are
dealing with this problem but they do know that some of the
people who support the SDI are also identified with what
they would regard as a somewhat neo-isolationist tendency
in the United States. They are worried about that because
they see that the SDI for this group of supporters, if it
becomes ascendant, might move in a direction which might
raise in a concrete way this problem of decoupling of the
American strategic deterrent.

Another question which relates more directly to what
the Europeans hope will come out of the newly-initiated
summits is whether the ultimate choice will be between arms
control and the search for defensive systems. In other
words, will the administration's commitment to the SDI lead
to a breakdown or stagnation of the Geneva arms control
talks? The Soviets already have been quite successful in
exploiting this theme in their propaganda campaign directed
against the SDI. I think that Washington perhaps is not
entirely aware of how strong European opinion might be on
this subject. If it becomes necessary to sacrifice the SDI
to save arms control, the average European, including
senior members of governments, would certainly be willing
to do that without second thought.

Chancellor Kohl who has vacillated on the subject but
generally supported the SDI has laid down a condition which
is that a space-based defense system must include strategic
unity. In effect it must cover all the alliance territory.
That is a big order and it is not quite clear that the

actual program as it has developed so far is really going
to be applicable, even conceptually, to the defense of
western Europe against the Soviet SS-20 missiles and the
other strategic missiles targeted on this area.

Last spring the British Foreign Secretary Sir Geoffrey
Howe made a rather astounding statement for a British diplomat when he said that there would be no advantage in
creating a new "Maginot Line" of the twentieth century li-
able to be outflanked by relatively simpler and demonstra-
bly cheaper countermeasures. He has not spoken publicly on
the subject since. I am sure Mrs. Thatcher had something to
do with telling him whatever he might think privately, he
had better watch his words. It is fair to say that despite
occasional public support that one finds in Europe on the
part of senior officials of various governments, privately
that support is much more lukewarm than it is publicly, and
in some cases actually amounts to opposition to the SDI.

Mr. Mitterand has been the most vocal in publicly ex-
pressing his opposition. At the last seven-power summit
meeting he refused to sign on to a declaration that the
United States wanted giving general support to the SDI and
in effect committing such European resources as might be
available to that support. The French have made a great
deal about the brain drain that might result from the SDI
program, i.e., that European scientists, particularly the
most eminent European scientists, would be stripped away
from their work in Europe and they would all be drawn to
the United States and to the SDI research being done here.
Of course the counterpoise to that has been his sponsorship
of the Eureka program which is to be carried out by the
European Community. The EC at a recent meeting of foreign
ministers and research ministers agreed on ten different
programmatic items that were to be addressed within the
Eureka program. The problem of course is that the EC does
not have enough money to fund that program at the present
time. However, these are indicators of the general trend of
European thinking. I would say that Mr. Mitterand has had
much more impact on European thinking than perhaps the
American press and government are aware.

The most basic concern of the Europeans is that somehow the existing strategic balance will be destabilized.
European governments, particularly ministries of defense,
are now raising the question of how this is going to affect
not only the basic NATO strategy of flexible response which
depends upon the extended deterrence of the United States
strategic forces, but also their future commitment within
NATO to the kind of cohesive adoption of common policies

which has been characteristic despite many internal battles
within the alliance. Another obvious question that they
raise is whether the technology of the SDI is purely defensive or whether it can also become offensive.

The Europeans are worried about the status of the ABM
Treaty. Generally speaking they do not get into the nice-
ties of the kind of legal interpretation or counter-inter-
pretation that the American legal community has gotten into
but they certainly do not want to see the ABM Treaty in any
way weakened or destroyed. There is a certain feeling that
it represents one of the few tangible achievements of arms
control in the last twenty years so there is a certain
value in retaining it as such a tangible evidence.

One thing that emerged from the European reaction to
Secretary Weinberger's sixty-day ultimatum was that the
Europeans feel that if they are to get involved in the SDI
at all, they have a right to be in on the take-off as well
as the landing. They do not want to be told after we have
made commitments and decisions what those commitments and
decisions are. They want to consulted all along the way. So
far that process of consultation has been fragmentary at
best and in some cases nonexistent. Nevertheless, the Europeans will insist on this treatment and one can only hope
that with reflection on these problems we will take into
account the European sensitivity.

There have been some uncomplimentary remarks made by
the SDI supporters about American diplomats. In some contexts these remarks might be accurate; however, in other
contexts they are misleading. If one does not assume American diplomacy has a role to play in this situation, one is
living in a dreamworld. American diplomacy has a very large
role to play. If we are to maintain cohesiveness within the
alliance, if we are to take account of these "peculiar"
European reactions which are rather strong and which are
irritating to Washington and others in the United States,
then our diplomacy has to become more adept, more supple,
and more responsive to what our European allies require.
This must be done if the cohesiveness of the alliance is to
be maintained and if the SDI is not to become instead of a
step forward in the strategic situation a five-steps back-
ward with consequent disintegrative effects on the alliance
itself.

9

SDI's Effects on East-West Relations

Colin S. Gray

I am reminded of the old axiom that a missile is strategic if it is aimed at you. You will have noticed that when Americans tend to talk about conflict in Europe and NATO strategy, they have a distressing habit of referring to Europe as a "theater". In other words, Europeans notice that we tend to think of Europe as a potential battlefield, as a theater for campaign operations. The "homeland/not homeland" distinction is basic to everybody and our allies do in fact notice that. I would agree that U.S. handling of the allies has been inept at least to the point of saying that perhaps we might have done rather better. And we are still in fact trying to find out how to do better.

My argument is that there is an explanation of the SDI that really relates to the real SDI as opposed to space shields and astrodomes that the European allies will find less offensive to their predilections than the SDI that they think they understand. We are somewhat confused in this country as to just what the SDI is about for very good reasons. We have this very intensive policy debate, debate about arms control strategy, but we do not yet within the U.S. government have agreement on what the military missions for the SDI may be. We are still at a relatively early stage of technical investigation. So a great deal of the policy debate is in a very important sense somewhat premature.

An important issue, particularly with Moscow as well as our allies in western Europe, is the thought that the SDI as a focused program of technical investigation looking at possible weapon architectures, as opposed to merely a broad-based research program, might just turn out to be a one-president excursion in American policy. Of course, regardless of who is elected in 1988, we are going to put a

great deal of money into research in this particular area.
But the notion of developing architectures, the multi-
layered weapons systems, looking to a decision for possible
early deployment in the 1990s, that being what the SDI is
all about could well go away with this particular president. This is the only president who is going to feel that
he owns this program. No subsequent president is going to
feel as closely committed emotionally as well as politically to the future of this idea of defending America as is
Ronald Reagan. This is why our allies and particularly the
Soviet Union are thinking about what is the reality of SDI
with regard to possible weaponization as opposed to merely
the troublesome things that we are actually researching.
Until 1989 or 1990 the Soviets do not know any more than
than we or our allies.

The SDI, and what the Soviets call by the rather different conception "space-strike weapons", are really the
flavor of the month. They are the flavor of the month for
commentary, for public relations. But one really needs to
think about strategic defense in some historical context.
The Soviets and our allies, indeed ourselves, can see very
clearly from the public record of American diplomacy, American policy statements, and American budgetary allocations,
that the United States is not about to forsake the known
world of international security relations with strategic
defense deployments in the near future. Weaponization is a
long way off, particularly as the Congress successively is
going to be cutting the SDI's nominal twenty-six billion
dollar research budget. We are going to find test schedules
stretched out further into the 1990s. Already senior administration officials and even the president are talking
about "my successor's successor." So this sort of magical
date when all the SDI research data will be in, the brief-
ing is held in the White House, and it is this nominal go
or no-go on weaponization, is a metaphor and a gross exag-
geration. For such a hypothetical moment we are no longer
really talking about 1990 or 1991. I suspect we are talking
very considerably into the 1990s if indeed at all.

The Soviets of course have noticed that the Congress
already has done considerable damage to the SDI research,
development, and test program with its budget cut for this
fiscal year. Given that the SDIO has already announced that
it plans to come in at a 4.9 billion dollar level next
year, one may make his own guess as to what the scale of
cut is going to be. So if we are thinking about big decisions for or against certain kinds of deployments at the
end of this decade or the very beginning of the next

decade, just think about the escalation of budget requests and what Congress is going to be doing to it between now and 1990. In other words, this is not going to happen quite as soon as some people appear to be believing or as the heat of current discussion might lead one to believe.

For reasons of domestic political appeal and for an American style of presentation, we have what we call a "strategic defense initiative," but of course it so happens that this initiative was triggered by our anxieties over Soviet offensive programs, triggered by presidential anxiety that we could not compete adequately with offensive nuclear programs. It also reflects concern on our part about Soviet defensive research, development, and actual deployment. The Soviets do have warm production lines for two operational missiles and several radars that would be relevant to very extensive deployments should they so choose to expend their national strength.

Also it is very far from plain that SDI is going to constitute anything remotely resembling a doctrinal revolution underpinning American strategic policy. At this moment we are still debating what the missions for SDI may be in a time-sequence sense, if we are talking about a revolution in American strategic policy, or if we are talking about reform of American strategic policy, about doing deterrence differently or somewhat differently or a little bit differently. We really do not know. A lot of the overexcited debate pro and con about mutual assured destruction is really beside the point. Mutual assured destruction is not American policy today, has never been American policy, and to the best of my knowledge has never been Soviet policy. The Soviets like ourselves believe in designing war plans to the extent that they can that make military sense. There may be some political value for intimidation in holding an adversary's cities hostage, but in terms of what one would actually implement in the event of war, killing Soviet civilians, like killing American civilians, is just not useful. From the point of view of the Soviet general staff or American defense planners, it makes no military sense. The SDI cannot challenge a MAD-based deterrence because such an idea of deterrence does not have authority in either superpower today and as far as I can tell from the historical record never has.

Weapons of all kinds are symptoms and not causes of political conflict. The roots of the Soviet-American antagonism or hostility lie in the nature of the Soviet political system which can be boiled down to being the anxieties of an insecure empire. On the reverse side it stems from

the power of the United States, as seen by Moscow, to or-
ganize effective opposition to the Soviet quest after total
security. In other words, it does not really matter whether
one characterizes Soviet foreign policy objectives as offensive or defensive. Our fault in Soviet eyes is that we
are too large, too powerful. Even if a president were to
engage in substantial unilateral disarmament, after he had
been impeached, his successor could reverse that process.
In other words, it is the inherent economic strength of the
United States that poses a basic, enduring threat to the
Soviet empire. I am making no reference whatsoever to ideology here; rather it lies in geopolitics.

Beyond the interest in preventing nuclear war, which
is a very substantial interest of course, there is very
little by way of common interest to provide a basis for
Soviet-American agreement, either a general political
agreement or, more narrowly, an arms control agreement.
Soviet-American relations allegedly were in a state of ten-
sion long before President Reagan announced his new commitment to the idea of strategic defense as late as March
23, 1983. So to those who are emphasizing today how the
well of political relations between East and West has been
poisoned by "Star Wars," SDI, space shields, space swords,
and the like, I say what was happening in 1979, 1980, 1981,
and 1982 before the White House rediscovered the virtues of
defending the homeland?

I would argue that, even much more narrowly with reference to arms control, SDI is hardly the impediment that
it is often made out to be to agreements that really are
worth negotiating. Soviet foreign policy behavior, or mis-
behavior if you care to be pejorative, the scope and pace
of the Soviet offensive modernization program, Soviet
treaty noncompliance real or believed -- these have poisoned the well for arms control long before the SDI came
along on the scene. A year after the president's speech,
Ambassador Gerard Smith was referring to some of the pro-
SDI claims about the impact of SDI upon arms control but he
was wrong because of timing. It so happens that SDIO, in
other words the organization to implement the president's
idea, was not created until the spring of 1984 after the
Soviets had walked out of the Geneva process. There was a
year between the president's speech and when directed studies were conducted. To say that the Soviets walked out
after the president's speech, which was not the SDI speech
but the strategic high-ground vision speech in March 1983,
does not tell you anything about the leverage and it is
technically wrong.

If anybody seriously believes that SDI in and of itself is a very important hindrance to an improvement in
Soviet-American relations, you should explain the attractions of the world that preceded the organization of the
SDI from the beginning of SALT I in 1969 until March 1983.
It is true that the Soviets are somewhat nostalgic for the
early 1970s, as well they might be. We had a discredited
president, a caretaker president, and then a president who
was generally held in the eyes of some to lack presidential
timber. That was the kind of United States which the Soviets thought it would be doing long-term business, not an
America riding tall in the saddle, even if the defense re-
armament program was not as efficiently managed as it might
have been.

What I want to suggest is that the Soviet quarrel with
the United States is not a quarrel over this or that weapon, this or that strategic policy, or even really this or
that particular president. Rather the Soviet quarrel is
with our existence as a very powerful state that threatens
realization of their interpretation of their security
needs. In other words, there is nothing an American president could do or say that would make a basic change in the
terms of Soviet-American relations. The Soviet Union is not
interested in political stability, save of course at home
and then, by God, is it interested in political stability
with a vengeance within the Soviet imperium! It certainly
is not interested in any variant of strategic stability as
we tend to define it. Indeed to even talk about stability/
instability in the context of Soviet weaponry is ludicrous
from the Soviet perspective. In Soviet eyes, stability/
instability is a matter of definition of who owns the weapons. In fact, to put it in the Soviet perspective, a trend
towards strategic stability would be a trend towards Soviet
military preponderance over all enemies combined. That is,
the stronger the camp of socialism the stronger the camp of
peace, a totally political definition. A particular type of
weapon system A as opposed to weapon system B, which we
tend to classify as a first-strike weapon as opposed to a
second-strike weapon, is not the way in which the Soviets
think about the world. The Soviets simply ask about the
world, "Whose weapon is it?" If it is a Soviet weapon, it
is stabilizing; if it is an American weapon, it is destabilizing. That is the beginning and the end of wisdom on
that. They will use western strategic jargon but that tells
you nothing about the criteria which move the Soviet general staff in their actual defense planning.

     I suggest that East-West relations and Soviet-American
relations in particular were bound to deteriorate once the
West regrouped after events of the 1970s to oppose Soviet
foreign policy. I believe Soviet officials are somewhat
nostalgic for the good old days of a severely weakened
President Nixon, a caretaker Ford, a U.S. Congress concerned to micromanage military aid, foreign policy to preclude immediate recurrence in Angola or Cambodia of the
recent failed adventure in Vietnam. That is the United
States the Soviet Union thought they were going to be dealing with. The correlation of forces was sliding in their
direction. They thought the objective factors in world affairs meant that they should be receiving more and more
clout for the military buildup in particular which they had
invested in over so many years and they noticed a loss of
confidence and a loss of nerve on the part of western gov-
erning elites. Who is to say, looking at the early and mid-
1970s, that they were wrong? The Reagan presidency came as
a somewhat unpleasant surprise in Moscow. The actual defense muscle that we have added might have been improved
had we had our priorities somewhat clearer. Nonetheless an
America which says "We are back" and a policy style that
was turned around almost immediately in 1981, even if the
objective factor of muscle really was not there, was a cir-
cumstance that the Soviet Union really had not anticipated.
     The Soviets know that in the medium long-term we in
the United States can do ourselves far more security damage
unilaterally by way of domestic politics than they can
achieve through competent negotiating in Geneva. In other
words, if SDI fails it is going to fail in defense politics
here at home, not because the Soviets did us in with some
sort of legal ambush in Geneva. In the Soviet perspective
the SDI does pose a high challenge to the quality of their
statecraft. On the one hand they certainly know, courtesy
of their own extensive research and development activity
and because of their respect (perhaps undue) for American
high technology-based industry, that the SDI is almost certain to be a very substantial technical success story with
regard to most military missions of interest. I am not
talking about space shields to protect every American baby.
I am talking about an SDI that, if weaponized, basically
does in the Soviet war plan as a war plan that makes military sense. We do not need 80 or 90 percent effectiveness
to deny the Soviets a strategic war plan that has military
integrity, that would achieve military objectives or political objectives on their side of the aisle. I have noticed
from Soviet publications, particularly the glossy pamphlet

the Soviets put out several months ago called "Star Wars: Dangers and Delusion," that there is an assumption that SDI, apart from the fully comprehensive, thoroughly reliable shield, is going to be a technical success. Soviet officials privately will say that they do not think that America will stay the course, and we can all agree that perfect defenses are unattainable. But these Soviets do not doubt that the American defense industry with some allied help can certainly make SDI a great success for military missions. The Soviets, to my personal knowledge and from what I have read, believe that SDI militarily will do what the administration says at the lower end of its ambitions it should be able to do.

So on the one hand they credit us with what looks to be a very threatening program to the quality of their strategic planning indeed. On the other hand they do have good reason to suspect that they can limit the unfavorable impact of SDI on their security if they play their cards right. They can encourage us to slow the pace of research and development and provide fuel to the domestic critics of SDI in the United States and in western Europe. This relates directly to the summit in Geneva and arms control in the very near future. While the political future of SDI and the momentum at home and in the alliance remains in some doubt -- is it a one-president excursion from policy as normal or is it truly a bipartisan national commitment to try and defend the country? -- so long as that remains in doubt, the Soviets are not going to provide any sort of evidence that would help bound the threat. They are not going to give General Abrahamson any arguments he can put before a critical or skeptical congressional committee saying, "See what we have just done in Geneva. I have a finite threat I can go at with my SDI." The Soviets will not give the administration those kinds of arguments at this stage in play because there are enough good reasons from the Soviet point of view looking at the politics and the economics of SDI here in the West for them to believe that we might just do in SDI ourselves. The Soviets do not want to help rescue the program from what may be very serious economic and political problems here at home.

What is more likely to happen is that the Soviets at some point, hopefully early in the next administration, are going to be convinced that the SDI truly is heading towards at least medium-term weaponization. In other words, it is not going to spin off into an endless research and development program; if not truly bipartisan, at least there is a very substantial national commitment to it. What can they

do if they think SDI is really coming at them, bearing in
mind the threat that SDI poses to a quarter-century of
strategic force investment on their part? The most obvious
option they have is to attempt a replay of 1972, i.e., a
diplomatic quick fix to a very severe military problem. The
ABM Treaty of 1972 achieved that for them. They were technically very considerably behind in ballistic missile defense technology in the early 1970s. They would anticipate
being behind with regard to many kinds of SDI technology in
the 1990s and beyond. Why not try and cut a deal with the
United States that will give the United States something
that will bound American ambitions? In fact the United
States may be eager if not delighted to bargained out of
some expensive options at that point in time. This would
bound the competition so that the damage to Soviet security
as they see it would be limited. The Soviets could try to
use the arms control process to buy time, to achieve something closer to parity in technical accomplishment. I think
we should expect them to do that. In fact there are one or
two trial balloons that can already be discerned in the
press from Soviet sources.

   It is a very serious element in American policy today
to say and really mean that we truly are interested in as
cooperative a defensive transition as may be negotiable.
That is, if the Soviets say, "Come, let us reason together"
about renegotiating some aspects of the ABM Treaty, there
will be a pounding of feet in the State Department and a
flood of cables from our European allied capitals. Given
the politics of deficit reduction over the next few years,
the incumbent in the White House at that time may be very
eager indeed to ask what they have in mind. The kind of
things the Soviets would like to offer us, if they believe
the weaponization of SDI is inevitable (as I think is more
likely than not to happen), would be by way of a massive
concession to reopen the detail of the ABM Treaty for discussion to permit a greater scale of deployment of ground-
based systems. In exchange for that, America will be asked
to severely constrain the development of anything related
to boost-phase or midcourse ballistic missile defense technologies. This is because the Soviets see themselves at a
long-term structural disadvantage in constructing a reliable defense technology that would work for boost and midcourse. If SDI is coming at them, the Soviets will work to
get some kind of veto authority over the kind of SDI as
opposed to the fact of SDI. Once they have granted the fact
that SDI is here, the operating question from the

perspective of the Soviet realist or diplomat is how to
channel it in the least damaging direction for security.

The SDI that we proceed with, absent undue damage with
congressional cuts to the development and test program, is
likely to provide a kind of leverage over the Soviets
toward the end of this decade and the beginning of the
next. The Soviets do not know whether this is a Reagan program or a truly American program. But in four or five years
from now the Soviets could be looking at a rather unpleasant future. They could be looking at a future where 70 to
80 percent of their offensive force's payload would have
extreme difficulty penetrating American defenses for useful
military purposes. Of course they could make a mess of
American society with perhaps many hundreds or thousands of
military explosions over North America. But to achieve
something useful in war for the Soviet Union for the protection of the Soviet homeland, even the early stages of an
SDI that is actually deployed would put the integrity of
the Soviet warplan in very serious question.

SDI is the kind of program which for the first time in
decades, if not since 1945, really would give us leverage
over the structure of the Soviet strategic program. They
would have to ask basic questions about the balance between
offense and defense. We must face the fact that we and the
Soviets share a rather important common interest, not merely in the prevention of nuclear war, but should deterrence
fail, in defense of the homeland. Protection of the homeland is not the radical thought in Moscow that it is to
some people in Washington. We could offer the Soviets a
deal in the 1990s that objectively would be very much in
their interests. I personally put in private to some Soviet
officials the question of why a cooperative defensive transition involving dramatic drawdowns in offensive forces and
free rein for defensive deployments would not be in the
Soviet interest, given that the leverage for us to achieve
that would have to be an alternative. The alternative that
the Soviets see would be growing military disadvantage, a
superior ability of American offensive forces to penetrate
Soviet defense and a superior ability of our defense to
keep Soviet missiles out. We would be offering them an arms
control deal that would be very much in the Soviet interest. We might even be prepared to trade what would be on
balance a superior offense/defense mix for an offense/de-
fense mix on the Soviet side.

With regard to the allies, our allies are not convinced that the wheel of deterrence is "broke" in Europe so
why should the Americans come in with yet another

technology initiative to fix something with which they are
quite happy? There are serious problems regarding the
possible strategy implications of SDI for Europe. The
problem is not really American SDI, the problem is
"SDI-ski". In other words the possible decoupling effect
for the NATO strategy does not come from American defense
as it comes from what may be licensed on the Soviet side.
We do have some difficulty explaining to the West Europeans
how they will be more secure in a world where long-range
nuclear threats would be at a very substantial discount. I
think we can find constructive answers. Indeed I believe
that SDI and Soviet defensive deployments would help drive
us away from over-reliance on the nuclear crutch which has
bedeviled for many decades and will help drive us to do
what we should have done for NATO strategy all along.

Discussion

Question: Various people have written that in order to deter Soviet aggression, or as you would call it "security-seeking," the United States should be prepared to initiate, dominate the escalation of, and eventually terminate on our terms, a limited nuclear war which would not reach the scale of deliberate destruction of cities. Please comment on the current thinking of escalation dominance and about how the SDI fits into this.

Dr. Gray: The U.S. government does have a theory of escalation control. The theory of damage limitation is not that in some dire, almost unimaginable event we would take out the Soviet weapons in a first strike or first use that could do us damage. It is that there would be, for reasons of mutual self-interest, reciprocation in targeting restraint. In some ways that physically is all we can do. We have no physical means at the moment for defending North America. The trouble with having an undefended North America in the context of our competition with the Soviets is that we have this enduring planned deficiency in regional defense capability around Eurasia which means that one of the bedrock notions behind flexible response and the NATO strategy is that it may well be we who need to take the strategic nuclear initiative. We would be initiating a first use of strategic nuclear weapons and our only hope that it would not end in a total holocaust for North America is that the Soviets would be almost as restrained as we were in our first strike in their strike back.

I am personally very unhappy with that. One among many reasons why I like active defense is that my understanding right or wrong of Soviet style in warfare suggests that a Soviet choice of a restrictive strike back is not the

91

Soviet way. I think that if the Soviets believe that a
strategic war is coming, let alone that they are actually
under attack, they are more likely than not to go early,
preemptively if they can, and to go very heavily.

What we are promising to do by way of beginning that
strategic escalation ladder is to begin a process that we
could not end. I have never quite understood how we achieve
the escalation dominance required to terminate a war on
favorable terms given the fact that our homeland is totally
unprotected. SDI plays in the escalation control realm in
several ways. Among other things, at least in its early
stages, it could and should help protect the last line of
deterrence, i.e., it should deny the Soviets a very effective preemptive strike if they believe that such a war is
about to occur. If we actually could defend North America
to a useful though certainly not preclusive degree, it
should mean that we would be risking less if we did what we
currently say we would do more likely than not in the event
of some galloping catastrophe in NATO Europe. Far from
leading to a Fortress America syndrome, if you are a strategic analyst, the defense of our homeland actually should
mean what would be at risk to presidential misadventure
would be considerably less. But the current notion that we
limit because the Soviets would exercise restraint in their
targeting I find very difficult indeed to believe.

Question: Part of the French Socialist Party proposed to
take the West Germans under the force de frappe shield. How
realistic is the European nuclear force, that the Europeans
defend the theater by themselves?

Ambassador Hillenbrand: This idea of a European unified
defense has been with us for a long time, ever since the
days of the treaty to set up a European defense community
which the French national assembly refused to ratify in
1954. I have noticed this comes in cycles. About every ten
or twelve years people begin to make speeches in Europe
about the need for a more unified European defense. The
French effort to revive the Western European Union a few
years ago, which has not gone very far, was part of this
recurrent effort.

If I were a European, the first question I would ask
is whether the protection of the force de frappe would provide the kind of security that the present system provides,
both psychologically as well as militarily. It is true that
the next generation of weapons, both British and French, is
going to multiply greatly the number of warheads available.

But the present force de frappe does not seem capable of becoming the basis for a truly viable and credible European defense establishment.

This is apart from the fact, of course, that the Federal Republic of Germany presents a unique problem in this context. I think it's quite inconceivable that any German government as presently constituted, and certainly as far as the other governments of Europe are concerned, would be very happy to see Germany go nuclear. Certainly the Soviet Union could be counted upon to respond vigorously to any such arrangement. I think that it is good that the Europeans think about greater political unity and so on but I think when they get into the military area they are beginning to swim in very dangerous waters. This would perhaps cause the very withdrawal of the United States from Europe which is the basis of European concern at the present time.

Dr. Gray: I think behind the French statement, indeed the whole notion of closer defense ties between France and Germany, is a somewhat distant French thought about whither Germany would tend, should the American commitment ever seriously waiver (particularly the forward-locally-deployed commitment in Germany). I believe that French policymakers thinking about the medium- and long-term future would like to offer West Germany a West European alternative to turning to the East. Obviously from a German point of view there is one capital in the world that actually could offer reunification and that is Moscow. I think from a French point of view, given the longer-term uncertainties about the American connection and European worries about neo-isolationist feeling over here, to continue to bind West Germany to the West and to deny her some of the attractions that some people in West German politics may see from a rapprochement with the East and reunification, the French are very concerned that France have some alternative home to go to. But I must say from a German point of view, the idea of being guaranteed by the force de frappe, given French priorities as opposed even to the very shaky promises of the United States, is an almost unimaginable one. Certainly you could not have a European nuclear deterrent without a single political authority. Western Europe is a long, long way from that single political authority.

Question: Dr. Gray, did I gather from what you said that you were thinking of the possibility of sharing SDI with the Soviets? If that is so, please comment on the potential

military spinoffs and the possible European reaction to
such sharing.

Dr. Gray: No, I did not say that. The point was made in the
context of the ABM Treaty. I know that some elements in the
British government are concerned that economic and techno-
logic participation in SDI now may have legal implications
in terms of the nontransfer elements of the ABM Treaty,
i.e., whether technology legally may be transferred from
American sources to British that would be distinctly chal-
lengeable in treaty terms.

    With regard to the applicability of SDI technology,
particularly in the data processing realm, the Soviets are
not just concerned about BMD, they are concerned about the
spinoff for air defense. They are very concerned about what
SDI battle management systems of all kinds may imply for
antisubmarine warfare. When you think not about the weapons
themselves but about the structure of what would go to make
up a multilayer SDI system, you realize that for many elements of ground warfare, certainly for antisubmarine warfare and air defense, much of what we would learn particularly in the data processing side would be very relevant
indeed.

Question: What I am concerned about is that no mention has
been made about the economic repercussions. With all the
trading of insults right and left and a conscious escalation of the war effort and expenditures, where do we stand
with social services, higher education, taking care of
other social needs? I am very much disturbed that we look
at only one scenario rather than one of common interests
which both the Soviets and we have in peace. There are many
other things we can spend our billions and trillions of
dollars on. Why do we always think in terms of confronta-
tion?

Ambassador Hillenbrand: I think the discussion today has
been limited to the real world in which we, unfortunately
in the view of some, live. I sympathize entirely with your
views as to what ought to be but that's not the way it is.
That is what distinguishes realism from utopianism in the
world. I would also say that given the enormous scale of
U.S. budgetary expenditures, those twenty-six billion dollars, if they are actually appropriated for the next five
years for the SDI project, are not going to noticeably
either hinder or detract from other desirable expenditures.
The budget reduction process is going to be across the

board but it isn't largely attributable to SDI. The whole
defense budget is obviously going to come under continuing
scrutiny and that's another aspect of the problem. So that
I don't think, whatever one may believe about SDI at this
stage, that the budgetary aspect is important in my view.

PART FIVE

Concluding Observations

10

SDI and the Course
for the Future

Dean Rusk

Some of us who are older can remember the wave of consternation and near panic that swept through this country
when the Soviet Union put up its first Sputnik. That was an
object somewhat larger than a basketball that uttered a few
beeps as it orbited around the earth. Shortly after that
came man in outer space and developments which have passed
imagination in some respects. But by 1963 the United Nations General Assembly, under the leadership of its Committee on Outer Space, passed unanimously a far-reaching resolution on what it meant to have man enter the regime of
outer space. In 1967, just ten years after the launching of
Sputnik, we had the basic Outer Space Treaty.

At that time our thought was that outer space would be
a great arena of peaceful exploration and cooperation between nations. Astronauts and cosmonauts were the "envoys
of all mankind" and entitled to assistance from any who
were in a position to give them help when needed. Weapons
of mass destruction were not to be orbited in outer space.
The moon and other celestial bodies were not to be subject
to national appropriation. This was a world of peaceful
cooperation.

Now one question that must be in our minds is: Are we
going to scrap that approach and to make outer space an
arena of warfare? One of the mistakes we made many years
ago was not building into the Manhattan Project a political
task force from the very first day in order that all the
political contingencies might be considered and reflected
upon as we went ahead with the production of the atomic
bomb.

I can imagine, and I think it is probable, that within
two to five years there will be a resolution introduced
into the U.N. General Assembly, very probably by a group of
nonaligned countries, declaring that the placement of

weapons in orbit in outer space is prohibited as a matter
of law. Now a number of us might be able to agree on how to
examine the technical aspects of that as a legal matter and
whether the General Assembly had any legislative authority,
but I think we could expect such legislation to be passed
by an overwhelming majority of the U.N. General Assembly.
Whatever we think of it as law, there is a political problem there. Looking a little further down the road, suppose
that the Soviet Union were to announce following the adoption of that resolution that it will not accept the placement of any space platform in stationary orbit above the
Soviet Union which has any weapons in it. And it will take
such measures as are necessary to prevent such things from
happening. What do we do? The president and Congress would
have a problem. There would be those who would say that
knocking down such a satellite would be an act of war. So
far that's still words -- what do you do? Are we prepared
to force a capacity to station several hundred space platforms in outer space in order to give effect to SDI? I
would hope that there would be those who would be vetting
the political prospects for the next ten or twenty years
very carefully and thinking about alternative developments
if we are not to be caught by surprise.

There are a good many of us who have some serious
problems about moving the arms race into outer space who
nevertheless support research. We need to give ourselves a
hedge against any breakthrough in the state of the art by
anyone else, particularly someone else who might be hostile
toward the United States. I see no way to verify a ban on
research. A person with a good mind and a slide rule might
be the one who comes out with critically important ideas
affecting the whole subject matter. But there is another
reason. I would like to see this research carried on in
order that we might discover in due course whether we have
anything to quarrel about and whether there is a problem.
John F. Kennedy used to tell us, "If you're going to have a
fight, have a fight about something, don't have a fight
about nothing." It may be ten years or more before we will
know whether SDI is technically and scientifically feasible. It may be that out of it may come other things which
might be more reasonable such as land-based defenses around
missile sites and certain key centers. I think that the
Soviet Union is on a poor wicket when they seem to object
to research in this field. They have been carrying out such
research for some time now. My guess is that they will
withdraw from that position which simply cannot swim and

that we can find ourselves discussing these matters from other points of view.

It seems to me that we must give some thought to the question of costs. There have been those who have said if you can get a defense that will protect everybody, then cost should be no problem. It's not quite that way. I was on the space council in the latter part of the 1960s and I myself helped to veto a proposal in NASA to launch a manned flight to Mars. That flight would have required a two-year roundtrip and the initial estimate of cost was around 200 billion dollars. As these things go you could assume that the actual cost would be in the range of 300 to 400 billion dollars. Some of my colleagues on the space council and I decided it would be for another generation to make the judgment as to whether the difference between a manned flight to Mars and an instrumented exploration of Mars was worth that much money. We do not yet have enough information upon which to make a real judgment about costs but in terms of putting hundreds of space platforms up there, hundreds or thousands of space shuttle trips to build and maintain such stations, we are talking about hundreds of billions of dollars.

There are those who seem to think that maybe somehow we could gain some advantage over the Soviet Union in this program. My own guess is that that hope is illusory. There are those of use who underestimated the Soviet capacity to build an atomic bomb, then to build a hydrogen bomb, to put an object in space, to put a man in space. I think that we have to assume that whatever we can do in such a field the Soviets can do if they decide that from their own interests they themselves want to go down that path and mobilize the brainpower and the resources needed for the task. And if indeed there are some points at which they need ideas or technology from us, it is ridiculously easy for them to get it by careful study of congressional testimony and technical journals and a little dash of espionage here and there. I think that the idea that we can get any significant advantage over the Soviet Union is illusory.

SDI will have an effect on the arms race in offensive weapons. I will not go into the details of the legal arguments regarding the "broad" interpretation or the "restrictive" interpretation of the ABM Treaty. During the Truman administration, the Soviet ambassador came into see Secretary Dean Acheson on a point and Acheson spelled out to him the United States law on the matter. The ambassador protested and Acheson repeated it to him. This happened several times, whereupon the Soviet ambassador shrugged his shoulders and said, "But Mr. Secretary, the law is like the tongue of a wagon. It goes in the direction in which it is pointed." Rather than discussing the legal argument, I want to get to the heart of the matter. We had put in about a year's staff work under the leadership of Robert McNamara on the ABM problem. Just before the Glassboro meeting between Lyndon Johnson and Premier Kosygin we put this rationale to President Johnson. The essence was that if either we or the Soviet Union began to deploy ABMs, the inevitable result would be that each side would then multiply its offensive weapons in order to be able to saturate or penetrate ABM defenses before the main strike was delivered. So LBJ went to Glassboro and he tried this idea on Mr. Kosygin very forcefully, giving Mr. Kosygin what some people called the "LBJ treatment." But it was clear Mr. Kosygin had no brief from the Politburo on this subject, that they had not really given it any thought. He did make one remark regarding how anyone could possibly object to defensive weapons, a remark which I would put in the category of the naivete of the first look. After that meeting the Soviets went home and did their staffwork and came to the same conclusion that we had reached, namely that ABMs would be a very destabilizing factor in the arms race and could lead to a multiplication of offensive weapons.

Would the same thing happen with SDI? It does not surprise me that the Soviets are now saying that unless we can find some agreement on the space problem, there will be no agreement on offensive weapons because in the first instance, their response to SDI would be to look to the capabilities of their offensive weapons systems. We can be sure that each side will look for those offensive weapons which can penetrate or evade the other side's SDI defenses. There are a number of those weapons already in existence. It is not going to take a great deal for either side to bring new such weapons on line. My hunch is that the science and technology of devising offensive weapons which can penetrate or evade SDI defenses is much simpler and cheaper than the SDI defenses themselves.

It may be that the Soviet Union will reach the point where it decides that the multiplication of offensive weapons on both sides is reaching a point where, despite SDI, it is in their own interest to try to put some ceiling on that race and even bring some of the inventories down. I hope we will reach that point, but apparently we have not yet reached it as far as Soviet opinion is concerned. And so we have to give some thought to the question: Would our deployment of defensive weapons on any significant scale

result in a great stimulation to the nuclear arms race? I
think it is no accident that six former secretaries of defense, both Republican and Democratic, joined in a statement urging the maintenance of the ABM Treaty.

There is another element which bothers me although I
may be too much of a country boy to appreciate it. It seems
to me that SDI will require prepositioning commands to fire
into computers and other forms of technology. I am not very
happy about that prospect. I do not have that much confidence in technology. We lost our astronauts to the most
expensive and well-tested technology we had, other space
shuttle flights were aborted just seconds before lift-off,
we have sent satellites up there that just kept on going
and we do not know where they are. All of us live in our
daily lives with a gap between promise and performance on
the part of technology. The rinsing mechanism on the wash-
ing machine goes sour, the television screen goes blank and
they say to stand by because of technical difficulties.
Only once in sixty years have I had a clock in an automo-
bile that would keep time. I am very dubious about the idea
of prepositioning important commands to fire into such
technology.

We have some major questions ahead of us that we cannot avoid. They are real issues affecting our daily lives,
affecting the fate of the world in many respects. But I
myself do not approach such questions in a spirit of gloom
and doom. In 1985 we put behind us forty years since a
nuclear weapon has been fired in anger, despite a good many
serious and even dangerous crises we have had since 1945.
We have learned during those forty years that the fingers
on the nuclear triggers are not itchy, just waiting for a
pretext on which to launch these dreadful weapons. If some
of you doubt that as far as the United States is concerned,
let me remind you that we have taken almost 600,000 casualties in dead and wounded since the end of World War II in
support of collective security and without the firing of a
nuclear weapon. We have learned during that forty years
that leaders in Moscow have no more interest in destroying
Mother Russia than our leaders have in destroying our be-
loved America.

Of course that is no guarantee for the future. But it
is a good platform on which to build and is at least a partial antidote to the doomsday talk that is so widespread.
People in think tanks, some politicians, some people in the
news media, and some professors can string all sorts of
words together and dream up the most horrifying scenarios.
But I cannot put my finger on a single real situation in

the real world today which is pointing toward nuclear war. The simple truth is that people in Moscow and Washington are not idiots, whatever else you might think about them.

I would hope that we could address ourselves to these questions thoughtfully and with maximum help from the scientists who must help us a good deal in understanding just what it is we are talking about and what is possible. I would suggest to my non-scientist friends that we try to distinguish the scientist who is talking as a scientist from the scientist who is talking as a politician because sometimes they get these roles mixed up. A friend of mine remarked about Albert Einstein, "He was a genius in mathematical physics, an amateur in music, and a baby in politics." Nevertheless the scientists have as much right to speak in political terms as any other citizen. But sometimes we need to distinguish whether we are listening to science or policy debate.

I hope that Mr. Reagan and Mr. Gorbachev will not waste time in exchanging ideological sermons with each other nor waste time in launching threats at each other because that can get to be dangerous. I hope that they would reach out to search for some of the great common interests we and the Soviet Union have. We and they share a fundamental common interest in preventing a nuclear war. No one in his right mind in Moscow or Washington could deny that. We and they share a primordial obligation to the entire human race because we and they are the only two nations who, if locked in mortal conflict, can raise the serious question as to whether this planet could any longer sustain the human race. Their people and our people are common members of the family of man, the human race itself, Homo sapiens. We as a species are facing increasing problems which affect us all regardless of ideology or nationality in such fields as energy, the environment, population, and hunger. I hope that we would continue a search for points of possible agreement on large matters or small to help to broaden those bases of common interest and to reduce the range of issues on which violence might occur.

I am not neutral on the long-range aspects of SDI involving the development and deployment of these weapons systems in outer space. Maybe I am a victim of my own past involvement in the great Outer Space Treaty of 1967 and my part in helping to launch the discussions that led to the ABM Treaty of 1972. But if you want my summation briefly it is that spreading the arms race into outer space is politically inflammatory, militarily futile, economically absurd, and esthetically repulsive. Otherwise it's a good idea.

About the Contributors

LIEUTENANT GENERAL JAMES A. ABRAHAMSON is the director of the Strategic Defense Initiative Organization, Department of Defense, Washington, D.C. He is responsible for the nation's research and technology programs relating to defense against ballistic missiles. Following his graduation from the Massachusetts Institute of Technology, he joined the United States Air Force where he has held a variety of assignments in aeronautical engineering and space systems. In November 1981, General Abrahamson was appointed associate administrator for the space transportation system at NASA headquarters in Washington. He was responsible for the space shuttle program and guided the program into the operational era. He assumed his present duties in April 1984.

SENATOR SAM NUNN began his service to the State of Georgia as U.S. Senator in 1972. A graduate of Georgia Tech and the Emory University School of Law, he served in the Georgia House of Representatives from 1968 to 1972. As U.S. Senator, he currently serves on the Armed Services Committee, Governmental Affairs Committee, Intelligence Committee, and Small Business Committee. He is the ranking minority member on the Armed Services Committee and the Permanent Subcommittee on Investigations. In the area of national security, he has been a leading proponent of a mutual guaranteed nuclear build-down between the United States and the Soviet Union as well as the establishment of risk reduction facilities to promote crisis stability.

LIEUTENANT GENERAL DANIEL O. GRAHAM (RET.) is the director of the High Frontier Organization which promotes the development of defenses against ballistic missiles. He is a graduate of the United States Military Academy at West

Point. During his military career, where he served in Germany, South Korea, and Vietnam, his decorations included the Distinguished Service Medal as well as the Legion of Merit with two oakleaf clusters. He retired from the service in 1976 as director of the Defense Intelligence Agency. He was a research professor at the University of Miami and an adviser to the 1976 and 1980 presidential campaigns of Ronald Reagan. He founded the High Frontier Organization in 1981.

KOSTA TSIPIS is the director of the Program in Science and Technology for International Security, at the Massachusetts Institute of Technology. He received a Ph.D. in high-energy particle physics from Columbia University and has been with the physics department at MIT since 1966. Since 1973 his research has been devoted primarily to scientific and technical questions involved in the assessment of the effects of nuclear detonations and nuclear war, and in efforts to limit nuclear weapons. He has conducted technical analyses of new weapons systems such as particle beam and laser weapons. He is on the board of directors of the Council for a Livable World, SANE, and the Bulletin of the Atomic Scientists.

GERARD C. SMITH is president of the Consultants International Group as well as chairman of the board of the Arms Control Association. A recipient of Yale undergraduate and law degrees, he served as assistant secretary of state, director of policy planning staff, and special assistant for atomic energy affairs for Secretary of State John Foster Dulles. From 1970 to 1973 he was the director of the Arms Control and Disarmament Agency and was chief of the SALT I delegation. From 1977 to 1980 he served as ambassador-at-large and presidential special representative for non-proliferation. In 1981 he was awarded the Presidential Medal of Freedom, the nation's highest civilian award.

ABRAHAM D. SOFAER was sworn in as the legal adviser of the Department of State in June 1985. He received his law degree from New York University and went on to serve as law clerk to Judge J. Skelly Wright of the District of Columbia Court of Appeals as well as Judge William J. Brennan of the United States Supreme Court. From 1967 to 1969 he was assistant U.S. attorney in the southern district of New York. From 1969 to 1979 he served as professor of law at Columbia University. In 1979 he was appointed United States district judge in the southern district of New York. During his six-year term on the court, he published about 200 opinions in a variety of cases. He is a member of the American Bar Association and the American Law Institute.

CHRISTOPHER C. JOYNER is an associate professor of political science and a member of the School of Public and International Affairs at the George Washington University where he teaches courses on international law and world politics. A recipient of a Ph.D. in foreign affairs from the University of Virginia, he has published over one hundred articles, papers, and book reviews in professional journals. He has served on the executive council of the American Society of International Law and is currently president of the international law section of the International Studies Association. He serves as a consultant to the United Nations, NASA, the Department of State, and other public and private organizations.

MARTIN J. HILLENBRAND is the Dean Rusk Professor of International Relations and director of the Center for Global Policy Studies at the University of Georgia. He received a Ph.D. degree in public law from Columbia University in 1948. From 1939 to 1976 he served in the U.S. Foreign Service in posts throughout Europe, Africa, and the Far East. He was ambassador to Hungary from 1967 to 1969 and ambassador to the Federal Republic of Germany from 1972 to 1976. From 1969 to 1972 he served as assistant secretary of state for European affairs. From 1977 to 1982 he was director-general of the Atlantic Institute for International Affairs, Paris. In 1983 he was awarded the Department of State Director General's Cup for Distinguished Service in International Affairs.

COLIN S. GRAY is president of the National Institute for Public Policy. He studied at the University of Manchester and Oxford University in the United Kingdom and has taught at the universities of Lancaster (U.K.), York (Canada), British Columbia, and Georgetown University, Washington, D.C. His professional background is in the study of United States, Soviet, and NATO defense policies. His most recent books include American Military Space Policy (1983); Strategic Studies and Public Policy: The American Experience (1982); Strategic Studies: A Critical Assessment (1982); and The MX ICBM and National Security (1981).

DEAN RUSK is the Samuel H. Sibley Professor of Law at the University of Georgia. Following his studies as a Rhodes

Scholar at St. John's College, Oxford, he was associate
professor and dean of the faculty at Mills College. He
served in the U.S. Army from 1940 to 1946 in the China-Bur-
ma-India theatre. From 1947 to 1952 he was with the Department of State, where he served as assistant secretary of
state for United Nations affairs and for Far Eastern affairs. He was president of the Rockefeller Foundation from
1952 until 1960. He then served as secretary of state for
Presidents Kennedy and Johnson. He is a member of the American Society of International Law and the Council on Foreign Relations.

Index